W9-BQT-293

10
Prescriptions
for a
Healthy
Church

Other Abingdon Press Books by
Bob Farr and Kay Kotan

Get Their Name

Renovate or Die

10
Prescriptions
for a
Healthy
Church

Bob Farr
Kay Kotan

Foreword by Bishop Michael Coyner

Abingdon Press

Nashville

TEN PRESCRIPTIONS FOR A HEALTHY CHURCH

Copyright © 2015 by Abingdon Press

All rights reserved.

No part of this work may be reproduced or transmitted in any form or by any means, electronic or mechanical, including photocopying and recording, or by any information storage or retrieval system, except as may be expressly permitted by the 1976 Copyright Act or in writing from the publisher. Requests for permission should be addressed to Permissions, Abingdon Press, 2222 Rosa L. Parks Blvd., PO Box 280988, Nashville, TN 37228-0988 or permissions@umpublishing.org.

This book is printed on acid-free paper.

Library of Congress Cataloging-in-Publication Data

Farr, Bob.
    Ten prescriptions for a healthy church / Bob Farr and Kay Kotan.—First [edition].
        pages cm
    ISBN 978-1-63088-315-7 (binding: soft back)   1. Church renewal.   2. Church management.
I. Title.
    BV600.3.F374 2015
    253—dc23
                                                                    2014046391

All scripture quotations unless noted otherwise are taken from the Common English Bible. Copyright © 2011 by the Common English Bible. All rights reserved. Used by permission. www.Common EnglishBible.com.

15 16 17 18 19 20 21 22 23 24—10 9 8 7 6 5 4 3 2 1
MANUFACTURED IN THE UNITED STATES OF AMERICA

Contents

Foreword

Ripe for Renewal

I recently traveled to England for the Wesley Tour to learn more about John and Charles Wesley and the beginnings of the Methodist revival movement in the Church of England—which, of course, came to America and resulted in our United Methodist Church as well as the other branches of Methodism, now with over seventy-five million members worldwide.

I learned about the haunting similarities between the eighteenth-century Church of England and the twenty-first-century United Methodist Church in the United States. Here are some of those commonalities I discovered between the Church of England in Wesley's day and The UMC in the United States in our day:

- ✪ The high economic status of its members (the sociological principle of "redemption and lift") separated them from the masses and kept ordinary people from feeling welcome or hearing the good news.

- ✪ Clergy often lived away from their people, focused upon their careers, and saw ministry as a job.

- ✪ The church used outdated methods of teaching and preaching the faith.

- ✪ The church and the clergy focused on arguments about morality rather than proclaiming God's grace for all.

- ✪ Music and liturgy were morose and lethargic.

- Passion for the mission of the church was replaced with second-hand support of missions and charity.

- Education of the clergy was valued over wisdom, common sense, and fruitfulness in ministry.

- The church worked hand in hand with the government and other social constructs to maintain the status quo of the society.

- Preaching was focused upon "the head" and not "the heart."

- Laity were excluded from meaningful leadership.

This may sound like a very negative and pessimistic comparison, but the point is that the church was ripe for renewal and revival in Wesley's day, and it is in our day, too. I already see signs of such renewal and revival today. Those signs of revival are the following:

- More and more of our congregations are feeding the poor, providing free medical clinics, ministering to the children of their communities, and so on.

- Our key leaders, including our active bishops, are focused on increasing the number of vital congregations.

- Many of our younger clergy seem more committed to the mission of the church and less focused on their careers.

- Words like *evangelism* and *renewal* are no longer seen as alien to our church.

- Many efforts are breaking forth to make worship and preaching relevant and lively.

- Ministry is using more and more of the latest media and methods of communication.

- We are trying hard to be a more outwardly focused church.

- Laity are leading the way in many of these positive changes.

Will our United Methodist Church in the United States find renewal and revival? I pray so. I have given forty years of ministry trying to help (including many failed efforts). I continue to see both a dying old church and a new church being born.

Learning about the persistent, prayerful, patient, and passionate work of the Wesleys reminds me that such revival and renewal requires many people working to achieve it. It also requires God's grace to fill us with such a Spirit. My hope is that this book will be your inspiration to continue the persistent, prayerful, patient, and passionate work of Wesley in your local church setting today. I pray, "May it be so, Lord, and may I do my part." Please join me in that prayer.

Bishop Michael Coyner
Indiana Area, United Methodist Church

Acknowledgments

We would like to extend our sincere thanks and appreciation to the pastors and laity across the country who were willing to risk and experiment to reach new people for Jesus Christ.

We would also like to thank our families for their support and contributions.

A deep thank-you goes to the original six pastors and one district superintendent that helped start the HCI process: Jim Bluc, Mike Schreiner, Phil Neimeyer, Brad Reed, David Stewart, Robin Roderick, and Robyn Miller.

We have a very deep appreciation for and to Rev. Dr. Paul Borden, whose teaching and sharing with us transformed our HCI process.

A thank-you to Tammy Calcote, executive assistant in the Office of Congregational Excellence, as well as the Missouri Conference office, directors, and staff.

Introduction

There has been a great deal of interest from individuals and congregations who desire to transform their congregations and their communities. The Healthy Church Initiative (HCI) process was intentionally developed for the Missouri Conference of The United Methodist Church (UMC).

HCI is a transformation process for church leaders desiring to grow their church and reach new people. It is a process that works best when initiated and supported by a judicatory system. The process could be done and has been done by individual churches, pastors, and lay leaders, but it's more difficult without the support of a bigger system around you. Either way, it requires outside help (i.e., conferences, dioceses, districts, or associations).

HCI Overview

As we began to write this book, we realized we needed a brief HCI overview as a foundation to understanding where the prescriptions came from.

We begin the process by putting both pastors and laity into learning communities. We found it was first important to open up our leaders' eyes to see church through a different lens, one where its purpose is reaching new people for Christ, and to create conversation and focus outside the church walls. Once the leaders have completed at least one season in a learning community, the church then has the opportunity to decide if they would like to take a step forward and consider a consultation. The approval of the church board is required for a church to enter into the process.

When the church decides to enter into the process, the pastor is placed in a peer-mentoring group with other pastors also going through the consultation process. Peer mentoring is led by an outside facilitator (trained by the annual conference), lasts eighteen months, and consists of spiritual development, leadership development, sharing of the journey of consultation, and mentoring one another. Once the church decides to enter into the process, the church also begins the completion of a self-study. The self-study includes such things as demographics, statistics, church history, financial reports, community study, pastor's DISC and StrengthsFinder test, and so on. It normally takes about three months for a church to complete a self-study. The church is also asked to put together a prayer team to pray for the process, the community, the unchurched, the consultation team, and so on. While the church is completing the self-study, twelve mystery worshippers are dispatched by an outside contractor (Faith Perceptions) to provide a detailed first impression of a worship experience. The congregation is also asked to have approximately 25 percent of the worshipping congregation complete an online assessment, Readiness 360, to determine how ready the church is for transformation and change.

A preconsultation workshop for the leaders and congregation is conducted about six weeks prior to the consultation weekend. The consultation is performed over a three-day weekend by a consultation team consisting of a lead consultant, a coach, and laity. On Friday, the team spends the day interviewing the pastor and key leaders with scripted questions. On Friday evening, the team conducts a focus group with about twelve to fifteen people from the congregation that regularly attend but are not currently leaders in the congregation. On Saturday morning, the coach gathers the church board/council to further explore issues or ask questions that the team needs clarified. The congregation is then invited to a five-hour workshop on Saturday facilitated by the lead consultant. The purpose of the workshop is to help the congregation see a current reality of their circumstances and what it might take to become a healthy/healthier congregation. It is also a time for the consultation team to hear more from the congregation.

On Saturday afternoon, the consultation team creates a consultation report. The report is the culmination of information from the self-study, interviews, focus group, congregation input from the workshop, board/council conversation, mystery worshipper reports, Readiness 360 report, and the experiences of other churches that have gone through the process. The report consists of the five key strengths of the congregation, the five top concerns of the congregation, and the five prescriptions to address the concerns. The report is usually four pages in length. The pastor is brought in Saturday night for a preliminary view of the consultation report.

On Sunday, the lead consultant preaches at the worship service(s). After the final worship service, the lead consultant presents the report to the congregation. For the following thirty days, the congregation comes together in town hall meetings and prayer to discern if they believe the recommendations are what God desires for the congregation. At the end of the thirty days, the congregation comes together for a church conference to vote. If the church decides (by simple majority) to proceed, the coach will walk alongside the pastor and congregation to implement the prescriptions. The coach provides resources, encouragement, accountability, and training.

Why the Book?

We have had many individual requests for these HCI consultations. We have not been able to respond to individual requests for HCI consultations. In addition, there has been a great deal of interest in the prescriptions we have written that are the result of an HCI consultation weekend. In this book, you will find the ten most common prescriptions that have been written over the past eight years in HCI consultations.

We are not writing this book as experts in church growth or transformation. We don't believe there is such a thing. In fact, if somebody tells you that if you only were to do these three things, then your church will automatically grow—you should RUN. Run to the hills! It is just not that simple!

To become a competent and compelling congregation in the twenty-first century is a very complex, messy, hard, culture-changing, and long process. It requires a great deal of prayer, endurance, hard work, dedication, risk, and tenacity. All this work is for people you may not know, a culture you may not understand, and a result you may not get to experience. So why in the world would we even try this process? In our eight years of church consulting, we have seen dozens of congregations move from decline or status quo to energized, mission-engaged congregations. These congregations have freshened up their buildings. They've created discipleship pathways. They have created new, culturally relevant, and passionate worship experiences. They have created cultures of radical hospitality. They have reached their communities like never before. There is not a week that goes by that we don't hear stories of churches or pastors who are unsure if their churches would still exist if they had not chosen six months or five years ago to travel down this road of transformation. We have found countless pastors finding their mission and passion again by attempting transformation, resulting in being reenergized for the mission field. We hear of just enough victories in a week to give us the drive and hope that there will be more victories next week in spite of the setbacks that come much more often.

We do not feel the need to restate the massive decline of the church in the United States and Europe. We have lived with both the statistics and results our entire lives. Most of our collective memory is a church in decline. Yet, Rev. Emanuel Cleaver II once said at the Missouri Annual Conference session in 2009, "When you are already on the floor, you can't fall further." The church is already on the floor—but we can pick ourselves up with the help of the Holy Spirit and give the world Jesus Christ. This is why we, the authors, put together a process that can help one church at a time become more relevant and missionally engaged. Even if the wins are few and far between, it is worth it. If one person comes to know Christ as a result of the transformation process, it is so worth it.

"When you are already on the floor, you can't fall further." — Rev. Emanuel Cleaver II, former pastor of St. James United Methodist Church in Kansas City, MO

We are writing this book for two reasons. One is because the HCI is maturing as a process in the Missouri Annual Conference after eight years of impact of reaching younger and diverse people.

See the report from Donald R. House on his full evaluation of the statistical impact of HCI over an eight-year period. Preliminary results indicate a positive trend in transforming congregations.[1]

Given that the maturing process expanded its positive impact, we have felt a need along the way to put in written form the entire process and share our experiences, both good and bad. Hopefully, churches can learn from both our successes and mistakes so that they might be able to take the next step in the transformation process. We have treated the HCI process as an open source. We encourage each pastor to adapt the process to his or her church and culture. If churches are able to adapt the materials to their context and become healthier and more effective, it's a win for everyone.

Our second reason for writing the book is that over the last eight years we have encountered a group of individual churches that wanted to do the HCI process. But because of their location or situation, they were not surrounded by a judicatory system (i.e., conferences, dioceses, associations, or districts) that could help them in the process. We deeply believe that without the outside help of a supporting judicatory system, the church is less likely to see transformation. Without the involvement and support of a judicatory system, it is also much more difficult on the pastors and lay leaders. So what we will attempt in this book is to capture and share the ten most common prescriptions given to churches that participate in an HCI consultation so that individual churches might be able to attempt this transformation process on their own. We have come to the conclusion that the ten prescriptions in this book are the most common and most important ministries to address. We believe most churches will find two or three prescriptions that could likely be helpful and applied to their congrega-

---

1. Donald R. House Sr., "A Preliminary Evaluation of the Impact of the Healthy Church Initiative on Worship Attendance" (October 2014).

tional setting. One can read the book and workbook, hire a trained coach, and move the ball forward. This book comes after more than eight years of creating and implementing the Healthy Church Initiative process. HCI started in 2007 with six United Methodist pastors in Missouri who desired to lead more fruitful congregations. Since we began the process, there have been more than 200 HCI consultations in Missouri and an estimated five hundred more across the country.

In those more than 650 consultations, there were congregations that didn't see transformation or growth in terms of statistics. However, we did achieve a great deal of ministry improvement changes in most congregations. We have been highly successful at intermediate outcomes: Church buildings look different. Leaders and congregations are having different conversations. Churches are doing different ministries. Churches are more aware of the community that surrounds them. But they have yet to make new disciples of Jesus Christ, which takes a good deal more adaptive learning. Therefore, your church could read this book and learn from the prescriptions, then work through the workbook, and at the very least change the conversations and begin to talk about "what if." If your church has already had a consultation, maybe it is time to revisit the process and write your own prescriptions. HCI was never intended as a one-time fix. It is not a program. HCI was created as a comprehensive process of *continuous* evaluation and improvement. Our hope is that this book will help you with this continuous process of evaluation and improvement.

> The church is an organization that must be led and managed....Scripturally, the church is also an interdependent and living organism (1 Cor. 12:12, 14, 20, 27) where each person has something to contribute (Rom. 12:4-8; Eph. 4:11-13) to the community's involvement in God's mission (Matt. 28:18-20; Acts 1:8). Such Scriptures indicate that healthy components (that is, people) are necessary to form a healthy organization.[2]

HCI is a process that includes five key strategies: continuous learning communities, laity involvement, coaching, consultation, and accountability. The HCI process is referred to in our original book, *Renovate or Die*.[3] The particular teachings in this current book are specifically from the consultation stage of the HCI process.

In our work in the Missouri Conference of The United Methodist Church, our own conference, and in assisting other UMC conferences and other mainline

---

2. Bob Whitesel, *Organix: Signs of Leadership in a Changing Church* (Nashville: Abingdon Press, 2011), 43.

3. Bob Farr and Kay Kotan, *Renovate or Die: Ten Ways to Focus Your Church on Mission* (Nashville: Abingdon Press, 2011).

churches in implementing the process, we have found many similarities in our churches. When we began, we thought that each church would get a unique set of prescriptions because it was obvious that each church is unique. We have all heard the frustration of going about transformation with a standard template or cookie-cutter approach. We all are reluctant to have consultants come into our church. We have certainly heard of consultants who apply the same exact strategies to every church every time. So, as we began the HCI process, we tried desperately to write unique prescriptions for each church. But time and time again, much to our dismay, we found the same prevailing symptoms. For example, if we had found a church that had an effective mission and vision statement, we wouldn't have had to write that prescription. But time and time again, we found the same prevailing symptoms (i.e., no mission and vision statement). Consequently, we found ourselves writing similar prescriptions (i.e., the need for a mission and vision statement) whether we wanted to or not. As a result of our experience, we easily accumulated over a thousand pages of written prescriptions in our archives. Overwhelmingly, there were ten prescriptions written most often over the years. After eight years of consulting, we became painfully aware that the same basic symptoms appeared time and time again.

For example, I (Bob) was asked early on in the HCI process to conduct a consultation in Oregon. I was concerned there may be differences in progressive versus conservative approach or difference in theology style or approaches. What I discovered is that regardless of the church's theology, whether progressive or conservative or whether more or less evangelical, the same prevailing symptoms appeared. The church was lacking a mission and vision statement. There were signage issues in the church building. The church lacked any community connection. Certainly, they had a well-respected, progressive pastor that was loved and admired by a nice congregation of 250 people, just like so many of our Missouri congregations. Yet it was still obvious that this congregation, like so many in the Midwest, would have to change how it did things in order to reach people for Christ. In order to be faithful and fruitful in the twenty-first century, the congregation was going to have to make many of the same changes in behavior that had to be made in congregations in the Midwest.

I (Kay) have had the opportunity and privilege to coach and consult with other mainline churches and leaders. These denominations have included American Baptist, Presbyterian, and Disciples of Christ. What I have discovered is that the common symptoms we routinely find in the United Methodist congregations throughout the country are really no different than the prevailing symptoms of other mainline churches. The pastors, leaders, and congregations are all struggling with the same issues.

It seems we all have the same United Methodist/mainline/modern church "disease" or inwardly focused culture that keeps our churches from reaching a new generation. We have created a "church culture" that is pervasive across the country; in churches of all theologies and sizes; in urban, suburban, and county seat settings; in traditional, modern, and contemporary worship styles. Regardless of size and location, churches have a hard time reaching out to people they don't know. We've taught people to "do" church but not to be disciples of Jesus Christ. Just talking about this is hard for some people. Even in the most evangelical churches, congregants still have a hard time meeting people they don't know. In our most progressive churches—those that highly value education—congregants find it even more difficult and maybe even offensive to talk about Jesus to people they don't know. They do not want to offend anyone with their faith. We figured out along the way that whatever disease we United Methodists are suffering from, most mainline churches are suffering from it as well.

So what is this disease most mainline churches are suffering from? The best definition we have read is Kenda Creasy Dean's "Moralistic Therapeutic Deism" from *Almost Christian: What the Faith of Our Teenagers Is Telling the American Church.*[4] This is a great book about teenagers, but it really applies to us all. We define the disease as teaching people to play church rather than make disciples of Jesus Christ.

In a sense, this mainline disease has led us to believe that if we go up to the church building and do religious stuff, we will become spiritual. If we send our children to church to do religious stuff, they will become spiritual. If we do church work, we will be spiritual. But we have found this to not be true. In the Western culture, we have experienced rugged individualism. In the Western Christian culture, this has led to a distinct emphasis on individual salvation. So once you have been baptized, what is the purpose of the church? For the most part, it became fellowship. As if the church is simply a place to hang out, develop friendships, learn moral lessons for life, raise kids, and wait to go heaven. We, the leaders of the church, had to devise things to do while we waited. We, the leaders, devised activities that were mostly internally focused to maintain fellowship and added some missions in the community and world.

While this worked to gain members in the 1930s, 1940s, and 1950s when the law kept other things from competing with church on Sundays, it did not necessarily create disciples of Jesus Christ. We United Methodists somehow

---

4. Kenda Creasy Dean, *Almost Christian: What the Faith of Our Teenagers Is Telling the American Church* (New York: Oxford University Press, 2010), 14. The term *Moralistic Therapeutic Deism* was first introduced in the book *Soul Searching: The Religious and Spiritual Lives of American Teenagers* by Christian Smith and Melinda Lundquist Denton in 2005. It is used to describe what they consider to be common religious beliefs among American youth.

collectively lost our corporate memory that John Wesley emphasized working out salvation within bands and classes (modern-day small groups) through church. This is a group approach rather than the more individual approach emphasized today. Salvation for Wesley was always a work in progress rather than being saved once or confirmed once and remaining in fellowship at the church while waiting for heaven. This has resulted in really nice people and great fellowship, but not necessarily disciples. In our HCI weekend consultations, when we asked about the church's discipleship plan, leaders could easily tell us about the chicken dinners, quilting groups, and other fellowship opportunities. They struggled to tell us about any faith development plans. If church is mostly about a place for hanging out in fellowship, then there are many other opportunities that offer way better hangout places than the church. If your eighteen-year-old son or daughter or grandson or granddaughter is choosing where to spend his or her hangout time, would they choose your church? Or would they choose some other place most of the time? In the 1930s, 40s, and 50s, there were no alternate hangout places. Today there are thousands of alternate places!

In *Organix: Signs of Leadership in a Changing Church*, Whitesel describes two styles of leadership: modern and millennial.

Modern leadership (primarily those born before 1975) believes that

○ "healthy people emerge out of healthy churches,"

○ "spiritual health results from a largely private effort," and

○ "volunteering in a large organization will make people healthy."

In contrast, millennial leadership (primarily those born after 1975) believes

○ "a healthy church is healthy people,"

○ "spiritual health results from a personal and communal effort," and

○ "volunteer health is a network of small groups."[5]

We have discovered that part of the mainline church disease can be traced back to the differences between modern and millennial understandings of life. Most mainline church members were formed in the modern era of organizations.

---

5. Whitesel, *Organix*, 42.

You will notice that modern leadership believes healthy people are the result of a healthy church, while millennial leadership believes healthy people make up a healthy church. Modern leadership believes spiritual health comes from a private effort while millennial leadership believes spiritual health comes from both personal and communal effort. Modern leadership believes volunteering in a large organization will make people happy while millennial leadership believes volunteer health arises from a network of small groups. As you can see, these sharp contrasts in leadership beliefs can create large divides in any organization, including our churches today. Having two or more key leaders that come from these two different leadership beliefs can cause clashes in agreeing upon vision, goals, and strategies for a church.

If we have learned anything in our eight years, we have learned this: the church is a living, breathing organism. It is not a corporation or a nonprofit organization. While we can learn from these two entities, the church is just not the same. We must tend to our living organism with care. Every church is unique. It is its own body of Christ. It is its own makeup of context, mission field, history, spiritual gifts, needs of the community, passions, personalities, resources, traditions, facilities, demographics, statistics, and so on. For all of the sameness, commonalities, and "mainline disease" noted above, churches are mixed in this organic, living, breathing organism of Jesus Christ. This is what makes this work so doggone hard! While there is much commonality in churches, that commonality is mixed in with uniqueness. How many times have we been in situations and looked at one another and said, "Really!?!?" This is what I (Bob) mean when I say, "Each church is mixed in its own sauce." Your church is mixed in your sauce whether you want it to be or not. It is unique. Yet, with all that angst, it is the way it is supposed to be. The church was always supposed to be a living, breathing organism (1 Cor 12:12-27). Whitesel came to the same conclusion in *Organix*.[6]

Prayer: A Must

One of the things we have discovered is that churches really struggle with how to invite the Holy Spirit and prayer into this HCI process. We have learned that if you don't, the process will never work. Therefore, it is absolutely essential to invite the Holy Spirit and prayer in first for any transformation to happen. To our surprise, when we asked churches to do this, many weren't able or willing to do so. Churches that did not figure out the prayer and spiritual dimension struggled with all the other parts of the process. Understanding the spiritual dimension of transformation and engaging the congregation in a life of prayer (personally and corporately) is fundamental in becoming more missional, competent,

---

6. Ibid., 43.

and compelling. Because this is most imperative, we have included the prayer process in our preface—not as a prescription, but as a fundamental and foundational element before even considering or entering the consultation process.

Step One

The very first thing to do before beginning the transformation process is to assemble a prayer team. This is not the traditional prayer team that concentrates on the joys and concerns of congregations. Rather, this is a prayer team that has an outward focus. The prayer team will be asked to pray for the mission field, for the unchurched in your neighborhood/mission field, the government officials (by name) in your community, the school principals, the firefighters (by name), the police officers (by name), the leaders of the church (by name), and the transformation process itself. This process must be bathed, wrapped, and undergirded in prayer! Take a look at Harrisonville UMC Prayer Team on YouTube and the testimony of their pastor, Scott Bailey-Kirk, below for inspiration.

In the thirty days preceding the HCI consultation weekend, the congregation is asked to do a small group study on prayer. The congregation is asked to pray for the process, the consultation team, the leaders, the pastor, and the community. The pastor then preaches on prayer in coordination with the small group study materials. This is a time for the church to prepare for what God is calling them to see, do, become, and know during the HCI process. A couple of the resources used are *Does Your Church Have a Prayer?* and *Remember the Future.*[7]

Step Two

In addition to putting together the prayer team, we often start the prescription implementation process with a day of prayer (healing and repentance) during the congregation's regular worship time. This is a time for individual as well as corporate forgiveness. It is a time for the congregation to repent for not being faithful to the Great Commission of making disciples of Jesus Christ for the transformation of the world. It is a beautiful service conducted by someone outside the congregation, allowing the congregation to put aside and forgive those people or things that might become obstacles for transformation.

> I believe that before any remedy (prescription) was prescribed, the most pivotal response on our part...was to pray. We earnestly became a people of prayer. I invited everyone each and every week to pray. I preached about prayer, I spoke about prayer,

---

7. Marc Brown, Kathy Merry, and John Briggs, *Does Your Church Have a Prayer?* (Nashville: Upper Room, 2009); Bishop Robert Schnase, *Remember the Future* (Nashville: Abingdon Press, 2012).

I instructed how to pray, and I prayed about prayer. When the prayer team began to form everyone felt "awkward" as we prayed for leaders in our community, prayed for our community, and then prayed for ourselves. However, as time progressed and we all got more comfortable in our prayer...God began to do something really awesome...and lives were changed. We prayed for space and found the old chapel was the perfect spot for prayer. So we cleaned it out and renovated the space into a beautiful prayer chapel. We met each week to pray for our community and for our church with a new enthusiasm and found great delight in "praying the space" where people would gather in the sanctuary each week to worship. As our boldness grew we ventured out into our community to "pray the space" for our bridge events and the space in the local park where we would host vacation Bible camp. We now ask people who attend our events how we might pray for them (they fill out slips of paper with prayer requests and place them in a prayer box). Over time...we have become a people of prayer. God has blessed us with a faithful and faith-filled prayer team and their actions have become contagious as so many of our church family have embraced a prayer life with new boldness and vigor. God has so richly blessed us in abundance that we have no choice but to share our blessing with others. —Rev. Scott Bailey-Kirk, Harrisonville UMC in Harrisonville, MO

Three Precautions

As you read this book and its accompanying workbook, you will discover we created it to be a self-guided resource for the entire HCI process. Let us offer our *first precaution*. While we felt called to share our findings, we would like to reiterate using an outside consultant and coach as best practices. We deeply believe in the need for an outside voice along the way. Most of the time, it is difficult to see the very things that you live with day in and day out. They have become "normal" or "usual." After you have been in a particular environment for six weeks, you become accustomed to the space and lose the outsider or new perspective. The longer you are in a place, the more comfortable you are with it. A consultant offers an outside perspective, a pair of eyes and ears that have proven to be very helpful, practical, and useful.

For example, we are doing some of our writing together at one of our district offices. This office is fairly new. We both remember our first trip to the building. You could easily miss the turn into the office complex. There are three buildings that look similar. Identifying the building is somewhat difficult. The directory is not in the vestibule immediately inside the building. We had to venture further into the hallway to find it. The building has a look and feel of dental and doctor offices. It didn't have the "feel" of the perceived church office. So we still wondered if we were in the right place. When we were getting close to where we thought the office should be based on the other suite numbers, it was still difficult to find because the sign was flat on the wall rather than being perpendicular to the wall. But once we entered the suite we found the office nicer and better laid out than most. On the second trip to the district office, all the things that bugged us on our first trip did not bother us on this trip because it became a familiar path. Each subsequent visit brought about more familiarity. This is our reality—nothing wrong or weird. We no longer see the oddities. It's comfortable. It's known. New eyes see and experience it differently than accustomed eyes. This is true of our churches, too. What is an obstacle for new folks is familiar and comfortable for we who have been around a while. Having a coach and consultant helps us see those possible obstacles and what barriers we may be putting up that we no longer are capable of seeing.

The second precaution is about accountability. Who is going to hold you accountable? I (Bob) will never forget about my travels to ten different pastoral leadership groups and continuous learning communities in Missouri to get feedback from the first couple of years in the HCI process. The participants in the groups had mostly positive comments about their experiences. But one issue stuck out more than anything else. The pastors shared that they were really just not very good at holding one another accountable. This amazed us given that we are the heritage of John Wesley, who was the king of accountability. He designed bands and classes to hold one another accountable. We human beings find it difficult to hold one another accountable. Given this state of the human nature, who is going to hold you accountable? We believe it needs to be someone outside your local setting. Without a coach to encourage you and hold you accountable, the church and its leaders will most times lose momentum, miss deadlines, get sidetracked by the urgent, and regrettably lose courage to complete the process. Without a coach, the church loses the opportunity for the benefit of outside resources, materials, best practices, training, experience, and referrals as needed to complete the process.

> We have learned that if you work the process, it will work. If you don't work the process, it will not work.

The third precaution is a warning that transformation takes time and can be painful. Remember, a transformation process is usually a journey of at least three to five years. It is easy to get lost and not complete the process. Transformation is a marathon rather than a sprint. We are impatient and would much prefer to have this be a fast process. Transformation is a slow, arduous process that does not come without significant relational pain. In fact, it has been very difficult for us to watch churches struggle through the process without seeing meaningful fruit quickly. It is sometimes two or three years post consultation before real fruit begins to grow. Yet, the pain of the consultation will arrive within weeks or months. Still, we continue to have people tell amazing stories of success in churches reaching people for Jesus Christ that are three or four years post consultation. We have learned that if you really work at the process, it will work. If you don't work at the process, it will not work.

We would encourage you to read this book and workbook as a collective leadership team because any transformation process includes risk. While the fruit is well worth the risk of transformation, the process does not come without risk, cost, and conflict (and hopefully a resulting victory) to congregations engaging in the transformation process. This cost may be incurred in a variety of ways:

⊕ Loss of those people who do not agree with the new vision

⊕ Conflict resulting from technical change and adaptive change as the church shifts into being more missional[8]

⊕ Loss of traditions held tightly by some

⊕ Leadership shortcomings being magnified

⊕ Struggle with the fact of the church having two mission fields: those of us already in our church and those in our community that do not have a relationship with Christ

⊕ Struggle to understand that our priority mission field must be with the community rather than those already in church

⊕ Shifting resources (dollars, people, facility usage, calendaring, and so on)

⊕ Creation of space for new people who may not think, act, or like the same things we do

⊕ Buried conflict coming to light

---

8. Technical changes address issues that people usually have the know-how to complete. These changes involve people putting into place solutions to problems to which they know the answers (adding signage, adding technology, changing decor, and so on). Adaptive change involves changing more than routine behaviors or preferences. It involves changing people's hearts and minds. It can threaten people's sense of identity and lead to resistance and even conflict. The answer to the problems that adaptive change seeks to solve are not necessarily known.

⊕ Cancellation of things that are dearly beloved and beginning of things we aren't comfortable doing

⊕ Loss of staff who are fine people but not effective

⊕ Possible facility changes

⊕ Change of worship times and style

⊕ Change of the role and function of pastor

⊕ Change of the role and function of laity

⊕ Change in use of individual's personal time

Radical change has radical costs. If the church is going to expect radical change, it needs to be ready to suffer some of the radical costs—truly, a Lenten reality! —Rev. Amy L. Gearhart, Missouri UMC in Columbia, MO

Book Organization

We have organized this book by the ten most common symptoms of our modern-day "playing church" disease, which we discovered through consultations over the past eight years. We have organized this book into ten chapters representing these top ten prescriptions. Each chapter covers common prevailing symptoms (signs), a prescription (recommendation), and then remedies (application) to address the symptoms. Each prescription is followed by one or more case studies.

Prevailing Symptoms

During the process of discovering the prevailing symptoms, we are looking for what is missing, what is malfunctioning, what is not engaging, what is obsolete, and what is a source of confusion resulting in the manifestation of the modern-day "playing church" disease rather than engagement in the mission field. We discover the symptoms by using questions and impressions, a form of appreciative inquiry. We ask lots and lots of questions! These questions and impressions come from the congregational self-study, interviews with staff and key leaders, focus groups, online readiness surveys, MissionInsite reports, mystery worshipper reports, a guided tour of the building, a board interview, and teaching workshops. In fact, the congregation at the end of the HCI weekend has a very clear, vivid picture of their current reality. Coincidently, 90 percent of the time the congregation correctly self-identifies their current reality and their prescriptions.

Prescription

A prescription identifies and addresses the prevailing symptom. A prescription is indicated for healing or improvement.

Dr. Paul A. Wright describes why he spent five years with Mother Teresa: "As a physician, I believed—and still do believe—that there must be some prescription or antidote to heal or at least improve almost any condition. . . . I sought out a specialist . . . [for] I suffered from a spiritual malady. . . . The name I kept encountering was that of Mother Teresa of Calcutta."[9]

A prescription is a concrete guideline (not the Ten Commandments, which were written in stone) with benchmarks, steps, and resources that identifies the team players and timelines for completion. A prescription addresses *what* to do about the prevailing symptom. However, it does not address *how* to address the prevailing symptom. The how is left to the team of people at the local church. The how is very different in each church. In other words, we call a play, but we don't run the play. A prescription is written to be flexible, but not negotiable.

The prescriptions in this book are actual prescriptions written by consultation teams. As you read these prescriptions, you will discover some inconsistencies, uniqueness, and particularities you might not have in your church. They were written for one particular church in a particular place. A prescription is a recommendation based on a particular concern in a particular setting.

An *R* with a slash through the right leg is a Latin abbreviation for "recipe," which has come to indicate a recipe or prescription for health. In the new leadership world the Rx serves as a fitting descriptor for a millennial emphasis on first addressing the spiritual and physical health of the leaders.[10]

Remedies

A remedy is the "on the ground" work or the "how to" the churches use to implement the prescriptions. The remedies include resources utilized to complete the prescription to overcome the symptoms. These include action steps, training, processes, readings, and so on.

---

9. Paul A. Wright, *Mother Teresa's Prescription: Finding Happiness and Peace in Service* (Notre Dame, IN: Ave Maria, 2006), 20.

10. Whitesel, *Organix*, 41.

Case Studies

These case studies are actual churches that experienced the consultation, were suffering with the symptoms, received the prescriptions, had the courage to follow the remedy, and experienced a shift in their congregations as a result.

Summary

At the conclusion of each chapter, you will find a summary. It is a quick recap table. The table indicates the characteristics of a compelling versus a non-compelling congregation within the topic of each chapter. It characterizes the perceptions of leaders, the congregation, and the community. It is a thumbnail sketch or review of the materials in the chapter offering the distinctions of a compelling versus a noncompelling congregation in terms of the prescription.

Group Questions

Also at the end of each chapter, you will find five questions. These questions are posed to help cultivate thought-provoking and productive conversations among the leadership team. This will help your team start discovering whether each particular prescription is a possible area of improvement in your church.

It is our hope that you would read and study this book along with a group of leaders. Then, as a group, decide if you could self-manage this process. If the answer is yes, then we suggest you acquire the workbook for your team and follow the instructions (although we recommend bringing in a consultant, coach, or outside resources). In the appendix, there will be contacts and a website where you can purchase additional help.

Mission and Vision

Prevailing Symptoms

The most common prescription written is centered on mission and vision. Usually, if there is a mission or vision statement, it is not widely known or understood by a large majority of the leaders—let alone the congregation. But let's be clear here. We have never seen a church grow by simply hanging a mission and vision statement on the wall. Many churches do indeed have one hanging on the wall, but it is rarely owned or understood by the leaders and congregation. On the other hand, we have never seen a growing congregation that didn't deeply understand their mission and vision. Not only did these congregations understand the statements, but they aligned their staffing, building use, ministries, decision-making, budget, and other areas to the mission and vision as well as well. Without a clearly understood and communicated mission and vision, the church operates without focus and purpose. Most churches we have encountered over the last eight years were driven simply by the calendar of events from last year and the year before that. Sometimes, because of the budgetary pressures, churches had begun to make decisions to start some programs and stop some things based on lack of resources rather than mission and vision. We often encounter churches that are screaming that they just need more volunteers or money in order to maintain the calendar of events they love to do. They believe that if only those in the congregation would volunteer more or give more, everything would be okay. Rarely are these decisions based on mission and vision. Rather, these decisions are based purely on trying to maintain what has always been done. Some of the churches were easily swayed to the latest, greatest "program" out of desperation, hoping if they did this then it would turn the church around. This very rarely works.

Though we have discovered that most churches' decisions are driven by multiple factors, rarely are decisions based on making disciples and living into the vision. The metaphor we like to use in the Saturday workshop during the HCI consultation to help explain this is "What or who is driving the car?" Just imagine for moment a 1966 red Mustang with four seats—two in the front and two in the back. The question posed is, who or what is in the driver's seat of the car? Who or what is in the passenger seat? Who or what is in the back seats? What we know is that growing, healthy congregations have vision (V) in the driver's seat. It is the key to everything. We also know the second key to growing, healthy congregations is having relationships (R) in the passenger seat. In other words, relationships are also a primary driving factor in healthy, growing congregations. These are relationships among members as well as those whom they don't know yet.[1] What is in the back seat? It is structure (S; how we order ourselves) and programs (P). Structure and programs are important in a healthy, growing congregation. But if structure and programs become the driver of the church, the church may be entering the cycle of decline, becoming less missional and losing track of its preferred future. We help people understand that unhealthy churches most generally have vision and relationships in back seats. Many times, we find that if relationships are in the passenger seat, those relationships are only among one another rather than also including those whom they don't know. So, at your church, what is in the driver's seat? What is in your passenger seat? What is driving your church? It could be personalities, calendar, theology, history, tradition,

---

1. In our book and workbook, *Get Their Name*, we offer an extensive process in helping your church grow by building new relationships. If your church is struggling with building relationships with new people in your mission field, you might consider a small group study to work on this.

the latest and greatest thing to do, money, facility, debt, and so on. It is important to understand and know this about your church now and into the future.

What we know is that competent, compelling congregations are driven by their mission and vision, followed by relationships with those they know and those they don't know.

Mission and vision provide a basis or foundation for the church's very existence. They provide unwavering focus and clarity. Without a clearly defined and understood mission and vision, the church and its leaders flounder. Without a mission, there is no basis on which leaders can make decisions, evaluate programs and performance, and hold leaders accountable.

We are quite aware that mission and vision are defined differently in the church and in corporate America. In fact, sometimes the mission and vision definitions are interchangeable and mean quite the opposite in corporate America or with some church leaders. For the purposes of the HCI process and this book we define mission as the purpose for existence, or the "why" we do what we do. Vision is defined as "how." Vision is obvious, strategic, and measurable. Mission is big, broad, and applies to all. Vision is more unique and particular to your congregation and it effectively and clearly describes how your congregation is going to accomplish the mission in its unique mission field and context.

Many churches spend days, weeks, and months trying to figure out the mission of their church when, in fact, that has already been decided for us as Christians. The mission is "to make new disciples of Jesus Christ for the transformation of the world." This is also

> We have never seen a church grow by hanging a mission and vision statement on the wall. On the other hand, we have never seen a growing congregation that didn't deeply understand the mission and vision.

true of most organizations. Usually, the mission is decided at the company or organization's birth and within their type of company (e.g., retail, restaurant, religious). For example, Walmart and McDonald's don't need to spend any time figuring out or thinking about the reason for their existence. Walmart doesn't try to sell Jesus. Churches don't go into the retail or hamburger business. When the corporation is birthed, the "why" is also birthed and remains constant. And often, the "why" is birthed before the corporation or organization has begun. Corporations change vision. Vision tells how they intend to accomplish their mission in their context within their culture today. In the past, vision statements were cast seven to ten years into the future. More recently, vision is cast five years into the future. But with the pace at which our world changes today, vision is now cast for eighteen months to three years.

The church was birthed out of Acts 2 with five purposes. These purposes are all the same whether you read *Five Practices of Fruitful Congregations* by Robert Schnase or *The Purpose Driven Church* by Rick Warren.[2] In addition to the book of Acts, we received the final instructions of Jesus Christ in Matthew 28:18-20 and Luke 9:1-6 with Jesus Christ sending the disciples out two by two to reach the new generations. We believe that God has already provided each church with their mission. We, United Methodists, believe it is contained within the Great Commission and the Great Commandments. We have summarized it into this statement: "To make disciples of Jesus Christ for the transformation of the world."[3] If you are going to be the church, your mission centers around Jesus's Great Commission.

Where we believe congregations need to spend their time is on working on their vision statements. Their visions articulate how they will uniquely live out the mission. Congregations need not get caught up in figuring out their mission. The purpose of why the church exists was gifted to us by Jesus Christ. Vision drives the church. Vision is the "how" of the church doing the "why" (mission). Yet we rarely find a church that gets this. They struggle with first casting a vision and most definitely struggle with living into the vision.

Visioneering *is the engineering of a vision. It's the process one follows to develop and maintain vision. "Vision," writes Andy Stanley, "is a clear mental picture of what could be, fueled by the conviction that it should be." In his book, Stanley builds a compelling case for the necessity of a clear, God-ordained vision for each of the roles of your life.*[4]

---

2. Robert Schnase, *Five Practices of Fruitful Congregations* (Nashville: Abingdon Press, 2007); Rick Warren, *The Purpose Driven Church: Every Church Is Big in God's Eyes* (Grand Rapids: Zondervan, 1995).

3. *The Book of Discipline of The United Methodist Church, 2012* (Nashville: The United Methodist Publishing House, 2012), ¶120.

4. Andy Stanley, *Visioneering: God's Blueprint for Developing and Maintaining Vision* (Colorado Springs: Multnomah, 1999), 18.

In order to accomplish the mission and live into your vision, your church must center everything around the mission and vision. I (Kay) guide congregations through strategic ministry planning. The five components of strategic ministry planning are mission, vision, core values, goals, and objectives. I (Bob) use the diagram below to help congregations understand how everything in the church is built on the mission and vision. The focus narrows as you move down the V. Every activity in the church needs to be strategic and measurable on how it is moving toward accomplishing the mission and living into the vision.

How will I spend time in the mission field at each level? If a pastor spends X times in the mission field, laity should be spending at least half of X in the mission field.

For The United Methodist Church, we use the mission statement, "to make disciples of Jesus Christ for the transformation of the world."[5] If you are going to be a United Methodist church, this is your mission. In the Missouri Conference

---

5. 2012 *Discipline*, ¶120.

of The United Methodist Church, we are convicted that this will be our mission, and we clearly articulate this in the HCI consultations. In Missouri, in the HCI process, we tweaked the mission by one word. We have added *new* in front of the word *disciples*. We found without adding *new*, many churches felt they were living into their mission by continuing to (only) develop the congregants already in the pews or reconnecting with those disconnected from the church. By adding *new*, the mission statement clearly defines that we are to raise up new disciples as well as cultivate growth in seasoned Christians.

By adopting a mission statement and fully living into the understanding, a church can become a "missional" church. A missional church is one that measures all they do on how effectively they are living out their mission (their purpose). Everything is centered on the mission. Leadership teams frame all their decisions and conversations into becoming/being a missional church.

To embrace the missional model, church leaders and members must shift

- From an internal to an external focus, ending the church as exclusive social club model
- From running programs and ministries to developing people as its core activity
- From church-based leadership to community-engaged leadership.[6]

Let us repeat again for the purposes of our work that we define vision as your church's unique approach to accomplishing the mission. It can also be defined as the preferred future of the church in three to five years. A vision very clearly provides a snapshot of how the church would uniquely look, feel, and act being missional in three to five years. Because the vision is a snapshot of your preferred future, the vision should be recast every three to five years. If the church is being guided by and performing from its vision, the church will have arrived at its "preferred future" in three to five years and a new vision is needed. Vision casting in a church creates momentum, energy, excitement, and alignment, and it legitimizes leadership and increases giving.

Prescriptions

Example One

On the day this consultation report is accepted (should that be the case), [church name] will adopt as the mission of the church, "The making of new dis-

---

6. Reggie McNeal, *Missional Renaissance: Changing the Scorecard for the Church* (San Francisco: Jossey-Bass, 2009), front flap.

ciples of Jesus Christ for the transformation of the world." This means that every ministry in the congregation must demonstrate how it will accomplish the mission and that new ministries need to have as their primary purpose the "making of new disciples." The congregation will have a day of prayer on or before [date] that will allow the membership to be fully prepared for the Lord's vision for the future of [church name]. The coach will conduct a day of visioning workshop to start the process of the pastor casting a new vision for [church name] that will be confirmed by leadership. The workshop will be conducted by [date]. The new vision statement will be completed by [date]. The pastor will then conduct a sermon series on the new vision for the church.

Example Two

On the day this consultation report is accepted (should that be the case), [church name] will take on as its mission statement, "the making of new disciples of Jesus Christ for the transformation of the world."

The congregation will have a day of prayer on or before [date] that will allow the membership to be fully prepared for the Lord's vision for the future of [church name]. The coach and the pastor will conduct a visioning workshop within thirty days of the day of prayer. The purpose of this day is to share in God's dream for working through the congregation both individually and collectively to reach this community. The church will seek God's direction to discover what percentage of the unchurched within a five-mile radius it is responsible to win to Christ and [church name].

A team will be assembled to work with the pastor to create consensus on this vision and to create a strategy to implement the vision in ways that fulfill the mission. This team will be composed of between three and five people assigned by the pastor in consultation with the coach. The new vision will be confirmed by the board/council by [date] and then presented to the congregation by [date].

Remedy

While the mission is adopted along with the prescription, it still must be communicated and lived into. Communication is key and can't be overdone. Mission must be talked about and acted upon over and over and over again. As we begin to communicate about it and act on it, the culture of the church will begin to shift. In the first example, the pastor is asked to do a sermon series on the mission to help the congregation begin to grasp the purpose of the church as being missional. Along with the vision statement, the mission statement is to be printed on all meeting agendas, bulletins, websites, or other media for the purposes of focusing, reminding, communicating, and clarifying.

Since everything is launched and centered on the vision, the visioning day process is usually the first step of prescription implementation about thirty days following the day of prayer. The pastor calls the congregation together. The four-hour event is led by the HCI coach. The workshop includes the following elements:

- Understanding of mission

- Understanding of vision and its link to mission

- Understanding of the importance of vision and what it does for a congregation

- Explanation that vision comes from the intersection of the needs of the community, the passions of the leaders, and the gifts of the congregation

- Community prayer walk

- Small groups sharing of prayer walk experience

- Sharing of other churches' vision statements

- Small groups drafting vision statement

- Sharing of vision drafts

The most powerful aspect of the visioning day process is most often the prayer walk. Often, this is the first experience people have had in prayer walking. Participants are asked to walk in the mission field as though they had on the sandals of Jesus. What would Jesus see, hear, notice, and experience? What would break his heart? What burden is Jesus calling the church to carry or bear in the mission field? We ask for this to be a solo event, not a time for fellowship. Repeatedly, I (Kay) have been privileged to witness the profound impact on the hearts of longtime church members as a result of the prayer walk. People's eyes are opened in a different way to their mission field. Hearts are broken, softened, and moved to be a different church for the community. There are oftentimes many tears and deep shifts made in the souls of those participating. This workshop does first speak to the "head" of the matter (understanding what a vision is), but it really gets to the "heart" (and soul) of the matter during the prayer walk. This can be a profound shift for the congregation in becoming a missional church. Again, make sure the prayer team is praying for the day of visioning participants and the mission field before, during, and after.

Notice the visioning process is not a committee-led process. Rather, it is a pastor-led, leadership-confirmed process. We believe a vision comes from the pastor's heart after much listening, research, prayer, and walk-around information (i.e., information gained by being present in and interviewing people in the community). However, no vision is a vision unless the lay leadership of the congregation confirms it. Vision of the pastor without confirmation by the leaders is not vision at all. It is simply an opinion.

We have encountered a couple of different scenarios in churches struggling with vision. In the first scenario, some churches believe the vision process is committee initiated and takes six to eight months. By that time, the congregation has moved on. The second scenario we encounter is a pastor having a vision from his or her heart without following the steps above (visioning day, listening, research, congregational prayer walk, pastor in prayer, and discernment and walk-around information) and without the lay leadership confirming it. The pastor is simply doing his or her own thing and quickly runs into trouble. We would hear things like the pastor is doing things his or her own way, his or her vision is not the church's vision, and so on. At the end of the day, people are unwilling to follow the direction of the vision. A word of caution to laity and pastor: a genuine vision comes from the heart of the pastor and must be confirmed by the lay leadership. Pastors, make sure you look behind you to ensure people are following! And laity, it is not your job to be out in front of the pastor on a limb when your pastor wants to go a completely different direction. When a truly, Spirit-led, biblically guided vision occurs, the result is a creation of trust. In contrast, when the two situations above occur, the church becomes distrustful, lacks unity, lacks momentum, lacks focus, and may experience conflict.

Following the visioning day process, the pastor is to take all the information gathered, any available documents such as MissionInsite, reflections from the prayer walk, and the rough drafts compiled by the participants, and go into prayer and discernment to cast a final version of the vision statement. In a couple of weeks, the pastor will emerge with one or two vision statements to run by the leaders for confirmation. It is possible that when pastors run the vision statements by the leadership that they might believe the pastors have lost their mind. The pastor should receive their feedback and go back into prayer and discernment to create a modified vision statement to run past the leaders again. It is possible that the pastor may need to go back and forth two or three times. It is also possible that there will be confirmation from the leadership the first time. This entire process should last no longer than one or two months. Once the pastor has a confirmed vision, it is important for him or her to go before the congregation to cast the vision in multiple ways.

We have to confess we are Wesleyan, and we believe the vision must be confirmed by the lay leadership of the congregations. We are a church that deeply believes in confirmation. A pastor may get an idea, but The United Methodist Church believes he or she must have confirmation to proceed with effectiveness. It is our Wesleyan tradition.

For access to the day of visioning workshop and other HCI resources, visit www.HealthyChurchInitiative.org.

Case Studies

Case Study One

In 2011 our Small Church Initiative (SCI) Consultation Report included three prescriptions. These prescriptions focused on vision, children, and intentional faith development. All three were approved by the congregation, and now three years later the majority of them have been implemented.

The most challenging and most helpful prescription was that of vision. And just as helpful and fruitful was the creation of a clear discipleship pathway (intentional faith development). The creation of a new vision for Pacific UMC has given the mission of "making new disciples for Jesus Christ for the transformation of the world" new "legs and feet." The process of visioning created a new awareness of the community in which our church is located. It created a conversation around why the church exists. It gave us new eyes to see our role as a church IN the community. As we imagine new ministries we use the vision (Pacific UMC will reach out and invite the community to WORSHIP God, GROW in relationship with God and to SERVE God's people) in the discerning process.

The new vision has been empowering. We renovated the chancel area to allow flexibility and creativity for worship. A new children's worship time incorporates children worshipping with their peers and a curriculum that encourages GIVING—giving of themselves in obedience, care of the world, care for each other, and care for their church.

The challenge has been letting go of those ministries that are not fruitful and faithful to the mission and vision. Naming the real focus of our ministry events challenged some of the long held traditions. Naming the focus of the annual turkey dinner as a fundraiser was hard for folks to understand because for some this was their time to volunteer. As a people in process, the leadership team continues to understand and see the importance of keeping the mission and vision always before us as we seek to be a faithful and fruitful body of Christ. From my perspective and a few of the others on the Pacific UMC SCI task force, the learning time we had with other leadership teams of local churches in the SCI process was invaluable. While sometimes the format of the meetings was a challenge, the collaboration with other churches and the information discussed in our own small group was both enlightening and encouraging. Thank you, Kay, for your leadership! —Rev. Dee Pennington, pastor of Pacific UMC in Pacific, MO

Case Study Two

Central to the success of the entire HCI process to this point (and into the future) is the naming of the congregation's vision: connecting people at life's crossroads with God's love and grace. The congregation now considers each and every person and their particular circumstances ("crossroads") as specific ministries are developed and persons are engaged and invited to be a part of them. —Scott A. Moon, pastor of First United Methodist Church in Maryville, MO

Case Study Three

It may be a bit premature to talk about the success of HCI and Palmyra UMC. Worship attendance has grown from 120 to 160. Sunday school/small group participation has grown. But it is not yet sustainable.

As part of HCI we were asked to pull funds out of reserves. Last year we spent $20,000 in addition to our budget. This year we increased our budget and plan to pull out an additional $32,000. Now as we are halfway through the year, we have seen an increase in participation but not an increase in financial support. We hired two staff persons and they are doing great work, but our ability to raise the resources is still a challenge.

However, the key prescription to me that has had the greatest impact was our first one. Prescription #1: Mission and Vision

After the visioning retreat, Palmyra UMC scraped its previous mission/vision statement and drafted a new one. Using principles in *Simple Church* by Rainer and Geiger and *Five Practices* by Robert Schnase, we created a vision statement that drives and defines the church. Our budget, newsletter, and bulletin all reflect the new vision statement, and it is beginning to inspire and guide the congregation. It has helped us focus our efforts on the mission to make disciples. Here is a copy of our vision statement:

The Mission of Palmyra United Methodist Church is to make disciples of Jesus Christ for the transformation of the world.

Since God created the family as the basic human community through which persons are nurtured and sustained, Palmyra United Methodist Church's vision for fulfilling our mission is Creating Christian Families by:

CONNECTING people to Jesus Christ through community outreach and relevant worship;

EQUIPPING people to become committed followers of Jesus through small groups;

SUPPORTING people in a community of joy, grace, and love through celebration events and compassionate care;

SHARING our love of Christ to bring wholeness to our families, community and the world through generous giving and ministry service teams.

Our goal is for every person to be connected in worship, equipped as a disciple, supported in the community, and sharing Christ in service.

We have reorganized our church around the vision:

CONNECTION TEAM for Worship

CONNECTION TEAM for Outreach and Hospitality

EQUIPPING TEAM for Adults

EQUIPPING TEAM for Youth

EQUIPPING TEAM for Children

SUPPORTING CARE TEAM

SUPPORTING FELLOWSHIP TEAM

SHARE TEAM

—Rev. Eric Anderson, Palmyra UMC, Palmyra, MO

Summary

	Compelling	Noncompelling
Leadership	Clarity of purpose	"I think we have one somewhere"
Congregation	Sense of direction/ progress, how-tos	Cloudy, foggy
Community	Signature known ministry	Unconnected, nonexistent

Group Questions

1. Are we clear about our mission and vision of this church?

2. Do we, as leaders, understand our mission and vision?

3. Does our congregation know and understand our mission and vision?

4. Do we align our staff with our mission and vision?

5. Do we have goals that are aligned with our mission and vision?

Hospitality

Prevailing Symptoms

For as much as has been written about hospitality, being friendly, and being open to new people, we continue to be astounded by how most churches across the nation are not very hospitable. I (Bob) have been a professional guest/visitor for more than eight years. What I have experienced is not even close to hospitable. Even in one of our own Missouri new church starts, I walked into a church in an elementary school and no one spoke to me. I walked in alone as a single man. Was this the reason I was ignored or was it simply that the church has not learned how to be hospitable?

I (Kay) many times use the example of a family reunion setting to help congregations understand the point of how guests may feel. It goes something like this: How many of you have experienced family reunions with your own family? How many of you regularly gather with your extended family? (Most often everyone in the room has had at least one of these experiences.) Family reunions are great most of the time! Because we are family and we gather together routinely, we have history. We have customs and traditions. We have stories. We reminisce. Just imagine someone who has never met you showing up for your family reunion or gathering. They wouldn't know your history, your customs, your traditions, or your stories. They wouldn't be able to reminisce with you. How would they feel? They would most likely feel left out, awkward, and uncomfortable, even if you were being very nice. This is how guests feel when they attend our churches the first (and maybe second and third) time. Guests feel that they have just crashed our family reunion!

I (Bob) use the example of walking into the Farr family reunion in Sedalia, Missouri. All my family members are nice enough people. But if a stranger walked in he or she would feel out of place. There is no way for the stranger to catch up with the stories of my family or all the history, happenings, gatherings. There is nothing wrong with that. That's the purpose of family reunion. The problem is that when a guest visits a church, they feel they have walked into a family reunion.

We aren't saying not to connect with the people you already know. What we know through HCI is that you have to work overtime to get your congregation to be hospitable—not to just have fellowship. In larger churches, we believe our greeters will do the hospitality, but there is no real connection. You can feel lonely in a very large group of people. While visiting a small or medium-sized congregation can make guests feel like they have crashed a family reunion, guests visiting a large church can feel like they are going to a rock concert, which is fine—unless you want to get connected with people and build authentic relationships.

In our experience in HCI, hospitality and the way we connect with people is one of the predominant problems keeping our churches from growing. This is key! If we don't get this right, nothing else matters. The ability to do hospitality and connections effectively is paramount. This is one of the keys keeping a church from being a compelling congregation and engaging with people. The habit of bad hospitality has been harder for congregations to break than we thought. Having a culture of hospitality and connection is indeed creating a new DNA of a more outwardly than inwardly focused congregation. It takes a great deal of effort, determination, and time to create this new culture.

Our mystery worshippers (people we hire to worship at churches going through the HCI process to give us their first impression report) consistently reported back to us that our churches are full of nice enough people but that they just didn't connect well. When asked if they would like to return to our HCI churches in Missouri (about one hundred or so congregations), at least 80 percent reported a no-return rating. They said, "No. No thanks." They would not choose to return. This leads us to a puzzle with most congregations. The congregations believed if they were nice to people they would return. However, our mystery worshippers reported that this was just not enough. People need to connect. The old cliché that people are aren't looking for just friendly churches but are looking for friends (relationships) proves to be true. Yet it is hard to break out of the family reunion feel and engage with others even though we know we need to do so.

We love what one of our church planters in Missouri, Matt Miofsky, says about guests. He says guests are using the "hang out" test. A guest comes in, looks around, and wonders if he or she can hang out with these people. If the answer to that is no, it really doesn't matter what the preaching, music, and building are like. If the answer to that is yes, it doesn't matter as much what the preaching, music, and building are like. Guests will be back! The task of moving the church from being inwardly focused on fellowship to outwardly focused on hospitality is huge. Guests will give you a little more grace if they feel connected, but no grace if they don't feel connected.

Yet, most parishioners go home each Sunday thinking they belong to a friendly church. In other words, their definition of being friendly is being nice and kind to those they already know in the congregation. But the congregation is missing the part of connecting with new people. That is because, as parishioners, it did feel friendly to them. This is where experiencing being a guest in other churches by both laity and pastors is very helpful. Go experience what it feels like to be a guest in another church. Did you encounter hospitality or a family reunion? Guests are looking for friends—relationships. It is simply not enough to be friendly. We must offer ourselves up for authentic friendships/relationships. A mystery worshipper once reported that the folks at the church he visited were "nice enough but I just never got the impression that they wanted to be my friend."

First impressions occur very quickly. You cannot get first impressions twice. There is a certain level of hospitality that is expected as a guest in any place. For example, in a restaurant, we would expect to be greeted, to be shown to a table, to be offered menus, for our order to be taken, and for service to be prompt and friendly. But what sets one restaurant apart from the others is radical hospitality. Radical hospitality is going above and beyond expectations. It is "wowing" people. In a restaurant, the going above and beyond might be an experience of exceptional service like food or drink being brought to your table without asking or the owner stopping by your table to check on your experience.

Reversing the lack of hospitality and connection is accomplished by creating a new whole culture that goes beyond a hello, a handshake, and a conversation. You need to create a brand new culture. This reversal is more than creating a greeting system. It places high value on those you have not yet met. It reorders your regular worshipper values from honoring God, feeding my soul, and befriending others to honoring God and placing high value on guests, which in turn might feed your soul. This new culture involves little things like signage, décor, environment, and the use of your personal time, commitment, and habits as a regular worshipper on Sunday morning. It involves reassuring new people that this is not going to be a weird experience. This even means putting a high importance on the parking lot ministry to reassure people that they are in the right place.

For example, I (Kay) was recently asked to present some workshops at a church in California. The church was in a town I had never been in before, so everything was foreign to me. Because the church was located in an urban setting, the buildings were close together, traffic moved faster, and it was more difficult to spot signs and addresses on buildings. My GPS got me to the address, but I still wasn't sure that I was in the right place because the name on the building was different than what I was given. Next, I wasn't sure where to park. There was a very limited amount of street parking. I spotted a small parking lot across the street from the church, but I wasn't sure if it was the church's parking lot. I was unsure where to enter, as it was a very large facility with multiple entrances. There was a metal gate that was only slightly ajar. I decided to try it. Once through the gate, I found myself in a courtyard surrounded by multiple buildings and entrances. There were no signs to direct me. I finally found a youth and asked where I was to go. She escorted me to a building across the courtyard. There I found two ladies practicing music in an otherwise empty sanctuary. When I apologized for interrupting their rehearsal, one of the ladies took me back across the courtyard to another building. I slid into the back row and waited for confirmation that I was in the right place, hoping my host would notice my presence. Now this was my experience in a place where they had an *expected* guest. If I wasn't being paid to be there, I am not sure that I would have stayed. What would the experience be like for an unexpected guest?

The other experience we have had in HCI is the lack of church leaders who think about hospitality beyond Sunday. We don't pay attention to building evangelism. That is, how are we extending radical hospitality for people going through the building the other six days of the week? We never think of hospitality for the multiple groups using the building throughout the week. There are sometimes hundreds of people using the church building every week, and we don't know it or pay any attention to it. We think that just because they are in the building they will "hopefully" want to come to church. There is no real relational connection. Remember, we are not in the landlord/tenant business. We are in the relationship business—connecting first to people to be the bridge for a relationship with Christ.

I (Kay) conducted a consultation for a church in another United Methodist Conference. During the consultation weekend, we discovered that more than four hundred people were routinely in and out of the church facility every week. Yet, there was no intentional process for anyone to provide hospitality or make a connection with any of these people coming and going. The church felt that just by allowing the community to use their facility, people would somehow find their way to worship or another ministry. There was no human interaction. There was no one greeting these people. There was no one praying for these people. We didn't even know their names.

In working with churches, we continuously see a lack of building evangelism, examples of which include the lack of both exterior and interior building signage, not posting worship times inside or outside, and the lack of personal contacts with those people using the facility. We don't even notice the people who are using the building and aren't already a part of the congregation. We also found very few people understanding the need to provide hospitality at events outside church functions (e.g., socials, potlucks, voting polls, Scouts, and bridge events), let alone any follow-up process with anyone who was new.

One of our challenges as a congregation is the lack of hospitality we exhibit when we are out in the community. It is sad that most restaurant service people report Sunday being the worst tipping day of the week. What does that say about us? We think about being friendly on Sunday morning at church, but are we friendly and kind out in our community? In *The Art of Neighboring: Building Genuine Relationships Right Outside Your Door*, one pastor asked the mayor what the church could do to be helpful in the community.[1] The pastor was looking for a task, but mayor surprised the pastor with his answer. The mayor said he didn't find a noticeable difference between how Christians and non-Christians act in any given neighborhood in the community. He told the pastor it would be great to figure out a way to be a community of great neighbors. The pastor was puzzled by his answer and was somewhat resistant at first. After all, he was seeking a task for his congregation to complete! But as the pastor began to pray about it, he was challenged to name eight of his neighbors. "Obey the second commandment," he heard! Much to the pastor's dismay, he was unable to name his own neighbors. Take a look at the activity on page 38 of *The Art of Neighboring*. How many of the eight boxes are you able to complete fully about your own neighbors?

There is no way you can invite people to come to church unless you have an authentic relationship with them first. Yet, this is how most of us were taught to invite. If you meet someone who doesn't go to church, invite him or her to church. I (Kay) often compare this to approaching a stranger on the street and inviting her or her to dinner at my house tonight. That person doesn't know me. He or she would think the invitation is weird or maybe even creepy. That person could quite possibly wonder what ulterior motive I had. The invitation would not be received as genuine or authentic because I didn't first have a relationship with that person.

It is hard to know just what to say to motivate people to create a culture of radical hospitality. Yet it absolutely critical! It is going to take a prescription for a church to create this new culture of hospitality. It is going to take outside help. It is going to take resources, training, and accountability to make it happen.

---

1. Jay Pathak and Dave Runyon, *The Art of Neighboring: Building Genuine Relationships Right Outside Your Door* (Grand Rapids: Baker Books, 2012), 18–19.

We cannot say enough about how getting hospitality right at your church is critical!

Prescriptions

Example One

The pastor will identify a member of the church on or before [date] to lead the hospitality and connections ministry. This individual will partner with the pastor and the coach to train and equip others to function in the roles of greeters, ushers, and connectors. This individual will read the books *Beyond the First Visit* and *Five Practices of Fruitful Congregations* by [date] and will share the key concepts with others on this team.[2]

Example Two

The pastor and coordinator of hospitality, in consultation with the coach, will appoint a welcoming task force of between five and seven people by [date]. They will review the worship experience through the mystery worshipper report and improve hospitality for the worship experiences and other major on-ramps to discipleship (e.g., Wednesday night programs, youth and children's ministries, major outreach projects, and so on). The strategy for creating and improving the hospitality process will be implemented by [date]. After strategies have been enacted, [church name] will conduct a quarterly review to continue improving their hospitality ministry.

The hospitality team will expand the number of participants on this team to at least 10 percent of the worshipping community by [date]. The coach will work with appropriate leaders to train the team in the key components of connecting newcomers to the life of the church. The first training will occur by [date], using the book *Fusion: Turning First Time Guests into Fully-Engaged Members of Your Church* by Nelson Searcy.[3]

The number of entrances to the facility is a complicating factor in seeking to greet newcomers. We recommend conducting a traffic study on people and vehicles to determine the best way to deploy the hospitality team and to improve signage inside and outside the building. This needs to include getting signage that lets people know to park in the garage (if applicable). This should be com-

---

2. Gary L. McIntosh, *Beyond the First Visit: The Complete Guide to Connecting Guests to Your Church* (Grand Rapids: Baker Books, 2006); *Robert Schnase, Five Practices of Fruitful Congregations* (Nashville: Abingdon Press, 2007).

3. Nelson Searcy, *Fusion: Turning First Time Guests into Fully-Engaged Members of Your Church* (Ventura, CA: Regal, 2007).

pleted by [date]. Additionally, the study should include recommendations for security and evacuation plans.

In order to prevent people from falling through cracks, the church will identify, invest, and utilize a web-based database (like Church Community Builder, a church management software) to help shepherd people through the welcoming, connecting, and belonging continuum.

Finally, the information desk in the lobby area needs to be staffed whenever the building is open. The people who sit at that desk need to be fully informed and excited about the church and events that are currently happening. A review of materials for distribution and communication about frequently asked questions needs to be reviewed monthly at the staff meeting.

Example Three

The pastor, in consultation with the coach, will assemble a team of six to eight passionate individuals by [date] to develop a comprehensive plan for significantly improving the hospitality of [church name]. The team will research at least three other church's hospitality processes, review the mystery worshipper report, and read *Beyond the First Visit* and *Get Their Name*.[4] The plan will be put into place and begin by [date].

Remedy

As we have worked with congregations, we have emphasized that some of the best hospitality people are the newest people. The gift here is twofold. First, few people have a memory of things that were challenging for them when they were a first-time guest. For example, people who were guests recently remember not being greeted or not being able to find the front door or the restroom. New people to your congregation have fresh eyes, fresh ears, and fresh ideas on how to create a more hospitable environment. Secondly, hospitality is an easy place for new people to connect, become part of the team, and create a hospitality culture. We know new people do best with new people. New people who are with other new people can begin to start new stories. It is harder to connect new people with existing groups because they have to catch up with the groups' stories and history. It is often easier to start a new group for new people than to integrate new people into existing groups. Hospitality is a great place for new people to connect in ministry. It takes the least amount of training. And, they still have the recent memories of being a guest themselves.

---

4. McIntosh, *Beyond the First Visit*; Bob Farr, Doug Anderson, and Kay Kotan, *Get Their Name: Grow Your Church by Building New Relationships* (Nashville: Abingdon Press, 2013).

If a congregation already has a hospitality team in place, our experience is that they lack training. Rarely has a church been given intentional training to greet well and connect with people. To ask a volunteer to show up and shake hands at the door is simply not enough. Hospitality training is needed for ushers (if you have them), the hospitality team, new people for the hospitality team, and the congregation as a whole. If we delegate hospitality responsibility to only the hospitality team, we are not creating a congregational culture that embraces hospitality. This is like delegating the evangelism responsibility to the evangelism team and not having a congregational culture of invitation. This is not to say we should not have a team, but it can't be just the team's responsibility. We could have a great greeter at the door, but a guest could still not find the church hospitable overall.

One of our most recent lessons has come from Rev. Jim Ozier, who strongly believes that two or three times every year a church should have a Sunday morning worship experience built around creating and embedding a culture of hospitality. This culture teaches us that each and every person has a role in and responsibility for creating that culture of hospitality. The hospitality team must ensure guests have three "touches" before they are seated in worship. Those touches can include such things as parking lot attendants, door greeters, connector (people designated to "host" a guest and help them connect to the life of a congregation), ushers, pew hosts (people designated to extend hospitality to those people sitting in a particular pew), and so on. The hospitality team is responsible for the expectation and preparation for guests each and every Sunday as well as any other time the church is open or the church is in the community.

Hospitality does not stop after church on Sunday. The congregation needs to exude radical hospitality each and every time someone encounters their church. This is not limited to Sunday worship. Radical hospitality needs to be practiced during Scout meetings, small groups, council meetings, funerals, voting polls, community meetings—anytime a guest comes into the building. Furthermore, whenever we do events in the community, we need to practice radical hospitality, too!

Hospitality training does not stop at the hospitality team. In order to create a culture of hospitality throughout the church, we at least need to provide annual hospitality training for the entire congregation. Radical hospitality is created by changing the DNA of our church. It is a focus on others above ourselves. Radical hospitality might be demonstrated by a Sunday school class deciding to meet another evening of the week so that they can make themselves available for radical hospitality on Sunday morning.

To prepare your church building and congregation to receive guests and to create a culture of continuous radical hospitality, see section three of our book and workbook *Get Their Name*. *Clip In: Risking Hospitality in Your Church* is also a valuable resource in discovering how to implement radical hospitality in your church.[5]

Case Studies

Case Study One

Hospitality was one of the first prescriptions that we implemented at Community. After visiting several churches in the state, both United Methodist and non-UMC, our HCI hospitality team began a process that is still going on to this day to provide for radical hospitality on Sunday morning and at other events within our facility.

Community UMC relocated to our current facility, a former insurance building, around seventeen years ago. As of 2010, the building still looked more like an institutionalized insurance building. Hospitality through ushers and greeters on Sunday morning was handled through volunteers with low accountability for service and lack of vision for being hospitable to new comers.

Immediately after the research of our HCI hospitality team, the entry hallway walls were painted a very warm and inviting tan brown that felt much more welcoming than the institutional white and blue. Signage on the outside and on the inside was vastly improved, which was necessary because our facility was very difficult to navigate without them. Our parking lot, which had not been maintained since CUMC moved into the facility, and apparently several years before that, was resurfaced, and a damaged western sidewalk into our facility was redone.

The biggest change to our hospitality ministry was with our people. It has been a slow process, but instead of a loose confederation of volunteers that were gathered through e-mail communication, we now have several hospitality teams with team members that are committed and excited to welcome people to our church. The hiring of a gifted quarter-time director of hospitality ministry who has excellent organizational and leadership skills has greatly benefited us. The feedback we receive from visitors is that when they come to worship or Vacation Bible School or any other event at Community, they feel that they are home. —Kevin Shelton, pastor of Community UMC in Columbia, MO

Case Study Two

The most visible results (from the HCI consultation process) have come from putting key practices in place to establish a culture that is hospitable. The rate of returning guests has practically doubled. Key practices adopted include:

---

5. Farr, Anderson, and Kotan, *Get Their Name*; Jim Ozier and Fiona Haworth, *Clip In: Risking Hospitality in Your Church* (Nashville: Abingdon Press, 2014).

- Attractive, easily identifiable vests were procured and are worn by greeters and hosts.

- Greeters and hosts are trained on a regular basis (three to four times per year at this point).

- Greeters are regularly scheduled to assist worshipers and guests at each entrance.

- A main host who oversees hospitality is present throughout Sunday morning.

- A fellowship hall host tends to hospitality between services in the "meet and greet" time.

- Sanctuary hosts are scheduled on a monthly basis to oversee hospitality in the sanctuary and handle traditional usher functions.

- Twice a year, the worship service focuses on developing hospitable practices among the congregation, via message, dramatizations, distribution of 5-10 Link Rule cards, and so on.

- Attention is provided to designing and leading worship to make the service "guest-friendly."

- Guests are met by greeters/hosts following worship to connect them with fellowship opportunities and classes and to provide a take-away (typically a bag of goodies).

—Scott A. Moon, pastor of First United Methodist Church in Maryville, MO

Summary

	Compelling	Noncompelling
Leadership	Hospitality is a priority	Hospitality is really fellowship
Congregation	Trained to be part of hospitality culture	Volunteers have got it
Community	Genuine connection felt	Inward focus—nice but not hospitable

Group Questions

1. What does your present hospitality look like? Is it a team or a one-person operation?

2. Is a hospitality culture embedded throughout the congregation?

3. Does the congregation feel more like a family reunion or do new people get connected?

4. Could you interview your most recent guest and ask about their experience?

5. Tell about a recent time when you were a guest in an unfamiliar place and how it felt and what your experience was.

Chapter Three
The Worship Experience

Prevailing Symptoms

In the real estate world, you will often hear it is all about location, location, location. In the church world, it is all about worship, preaching, and location. This is the fuel that makes the engine run. Just as the economy of our country was at the apex of healthiness during Bill Clinton's presidency, he was known to say, "It's the economy, stupid." In our church, one might say, "It's the worship, stupid!" Worship is the energy, sparkplug, or fuel of everything in the church. I challenge you to find a church that has poor worship where everything is great. However, you may find a church with great worship without other things going well. But we have no examples of the former. As goes worship, so goes everything else. If worship sucks, it's hard to get anything else going! You can't walk out of worship feeling lifeless and somehow think the rest of the ministries throughout the week are going to be engaging. If worship is energetic and well done, there is a very high likelihood that this is also a reflection of how everything else goes in the church. In other words, worship (fuel) is driving the church, and it's the initial item to create energy, which in turn spills over to everything else. Worship is the inspiration for the congregation. Jesus went to the temple, too, as a twelve-year-old boy (see Luke 2:39-52).

As goes worship, so goes everything else.

When people have good worship experiences, they are moved. They think, "Wow. This must be what heaven is like." They feel like they have experienced the presence of God. When it's great, it works like nothing else. Great worship and preaching can cause people to overlook many other things, such as less than adequate or crowded facilities or a lack of programs. Yet, it is hard to find these good worship experiences.

Good worship is just hard to find. We most often experience poor worship. While we would love to debunk this myth, we find poor worship time and time again. We sometimes even hear district superintendents talk about their worship experiences. District superintendents in The United Methodist Church spend their time worshipping each week with different churches in their district. More often than not, they walk about feeling discouraged after encountering poor worship time and time again.

Good worship is measured by all sorts of differing criteria. Yet, it isn't measured by what we might think. It is not all about theology. It is not all about music genre. It is not all about size. It is not all about a particular style. In our opinion, there is nothing worse than bad contemporary worship. There is nothing worse than traditional services with traditional music with songs people can't sing. Note: I (Bob) believe that not every song in our hymnal is meant to be sung. They are there as a witness to the past and for their theology, but they should not to be sung.

In our experiences during consultations as well as being guests in worship all over the country, we can't tell you how many times pastors ask what we think about their worship. And we are sorry to report that sometimes the most gracious thing we can say is, "It wasn't very good." We often encounter worship that is boring, is not inspirational, is lackadaisical, is lifeless, doesn't touch the heart, doesn't evoke emotion, lacks connection to life, has no life application, is routine, is scripted, lacks opportunity for the Holy Spirit to flow, and lacks a theme, just to name a few of our experiences. In fact, one church was so stuck in their worship experience that there was a laminated order of worship on the pulpit and lectern. Now, folks, that is being stuck in a rut! To be clear, we are not against using liturgy or practicing worship for reasons of excellence, but we are suggesting that there needs to be some room for flexibility, creativity, and excitement!

In the beginning, we did the whole weekend consultation and then experienced worship at the end. We never did address worship before the consultation report was written. Because of our worship experiences, we brought the mystery worshippers into the process. We needed an outside perspective of the worship prior to the consultation weekend.

Sunday morning still seems to be the prime time for worship. In our consulting experience, church people often believe unchurched people want to attend worship at a time other than Sunday morning. Yet, it is our experience that if a guest comes onto the property, it is still most likely to be during the Sunday morning timeframe. The prime time stills seems to be from 9:00 to 10:30 a.m. There may be thriving worship on Saturday night or Sunday night or even a weeknight worship experience. But without exception, we haven't found a church that doesn't have an anchor service on Sunday morning. This is our experience primarily gathered in the Midwest; your context may be different.

For millennials and perhaps most unchurched, the worship experience starts when the worshippers leave their homes and doesn't end until they return home. This mindset helps our existing parishioners to understand why our guests will only give us an hour. In the minds of the parishioners, the experience takes two or three hours. For a guest, it seems like they are giving up their entire morning.

My (Bob) Kansas City Chiefs' experience is a great example of how the commitment of time plays into the value people perceive in a given situation. I was a season ticket holder for twenty-five years. I love those Chiefs! In fact, I often say that I gave my kids more of a Chiefs' spirit than the Spirit of Jesus. When I was planting my first church in the Kansas City area, it was a ten-minute commute to the stadium and about a three-hour onsite experience. Once I moved to the St. Louis area, the distance to the stadium grew to a three-hour drive one way. It became an all-day experience to attend a Chiefs' game. After the second season of commuting to Kansas City for Chiefs' games, it became a difficult decision. I wasn't making a decision about investing three hours of my day to attend a game—I was making an all-day commitment and investment. I realized I was having a difficult time committing to all day, especially when the Chiefs weren't having winning seasons. I also realized that because of the long commute, I was only there for the game. I was no longer enjoying the whole Chiefs' experience of tailgating before the game and celebrating in the parking lot afterwards. (This would be like going to church without going to Sunday school or socializing before or after church.) Going to Kansas City for a Chiefs game became at least a nine-hour commitment—not three or four. The decision was now based on giving up the whole day to watch the Chiefs lose. Furthermore, I decided that if I was going to give up the whole day, at least I wanted a good experience while there. In the 1990s, the Chiefs were competitive and fun. Then it moved away from that experience. The Chiefs repeatedly lost. Morale was poor. The experience no longer matched the experiences in the '90s. I found the answer to attending or not was more often no rather than yes. After three seasons of this, I gave up the tickets.

This is what guests do. They don't get up on Sunday morning wondering how they will spend their time that day. The bigger question they have to consider is, "Do I want to give up three or more hours of my day?" Then, at church, we are left wondering why they didn't participate in Sunday school or the potluck after church. If the experience of worship is good, they may be more likely to come to your pregame activities or postgame celebration. If the worship itself is bad, they may not attend the surrounding events. I (Bob) didn't call and tell the Chiefs I wasn't coming back. I just didn't renew. It took the Chiefs a year to notice and send me a letter.

Does this sound like the church? The product on the field was terrible, the Chiefs didn't seem to care, and nobody seemed to notice I was no longer attending. Finally, the Chiefs talked me into a five-game pack, and they didn't win the games. So the product wasn't better, so again I didn't renew. Now they call every year to ask me to try again. I will watch and see if it gets better before I decide to invest again onsite. I will test and try them from afar. It is still an all-day commitment, which makes the sell even harder. This whole story sounds like our churches in a nonchurch culture.

Does your church have an online presence that potential visitors check out? The first step guests take to check out your church is not attending worship. They normally check out your church online first. This could include your website, Facebook, Instagram, and Twitter. After you pass the online test, another place for a first connection may be a fun community event. One of the church planters we work with in Missouri was recently perplexed by this online connection phenomenon. This particular pastor does a "coffee with the pastor" each Tuesday at a local restaurant. While at one of these regular coffees, a guy came up to him and started a conversation. The pastor asked the obvious questions (e.g., "What's your name?"; "What brought you to the church?"; "What do you like about the church?"; "How can we be helpful?"). The pastor finally admitted apologetically that he did not recognize the man. The man explained that he had attended worship six months ago, but he and his wife had to leave worship early so his wife could get to work, and that made him feel weird about walking out of worship early. So ever since then they had been watching online. What was perplexing for the church planter was how someone could be in relationship with the church for six months without the church knowing. The guy has been watching from afar. He was visiting the "front porch" of the church (online) at a safe distance. This is the place that he felt most comfortable. He wasn't comfortable getting any closer. In today's virtual world, we are being challenged by those watching us from afar. How we can connect with them?

As a church, you have to do four things really well on Sunday morning. These four important items are worship, hospitality, children's ministries, and engagement with the community via social media. So, remember, the worship experience is not just about the one-hour worship time. The worship experience starts when the worshipper leaves home and doesn't end until he or she returns home. How well that experience went lingers in the guest's mind and heart for a very long time. This is why every Sunday morning is crucial—not just one Sunday or a special Sunday. You have fifty-two events you need to pull off with excellence each year. Ken Callahan suggests that at the very least you need to have ten major Sundays each year.[1] The worship experience encompasses everything from finding the church online, navigating by car to find the church, parking, how guests are greeted, how soon they are greeted, how many times they are greeted, the worship itself, and then the postworship experience (the fifteen or so minutes following the conclusion of worship). As churches, we are sometimes shortsighted in thinking about a guest's experience only from the time the worship service starts and stops. We must open our minds and hearts to the fact that the worship experience is much more expansive than this.

The mystery worshipper report is a critical tool for us in knowing how the worship experience is going. This is a report compiled from the impressions of twelve different unchurched people from the community who were paid to attend worship (each on a different Sunday) and complete a survey about their experience. Some of the common initial issues reported from the mystery worshippers include having trouble navigating the church website, difficulty figuring out which door to enter, difficulty navigating the building, no one speaking to them, and the like. Once worship begins, they commonly report concerns in the style or tempo of the music, not being able to follow along or understand part of the worship service, greeting (or passing the peace) taking too long, and so on. The after-worship experience may be the most overlooked area in most churches. Most of the time, churches were paying no attention to the guest's experience after worship. Most people would tell you that if they had a good experience with something, they would like to share the experience with somebody. Yet, our regular attenders are making a beeline to the car and don't have guests on their radar.

In fact, I (Bob) had a recent experience in which some helpful folks were actually folding up the chairs before people were even out of them! The chairs were literally being pulled out from under them! While it was most likely not the impression these folks were trying to make, guests felt like they were being rushed out. Hang-around time is often missed for most churches. If folks are still hanging around after church, it is usually a good sign that things are going well. On the other hand, if five minutes after worship the building is empty, things aren't going well. Once worship concludes, we church people go about making lunch plans with one another, and we forget about the guests who are present. We leave them to find their own way out. We miss the opportunity to connect with guests and open up possible next steps.

---

1. Ken Callahan, *Twelve Keys to an Effective Church: Strong, Healthy Congregations Living in the Grace of God* (Hoboken, NJ: Jossey-Bass, 2010), 26.

We hired a company from Cape Girardeau, Missouri, Faith Perceptions. Together we created a survey with sixteen categories.

The first impressions rated by the mystery worshippers by Faith Perceptions (the company we use for mystery worshippers; see Appendix or website for more information) include the following:

COMMUNITY AWARENESS: Rates the community awareness of the church

SIGNAGE: Rates the effectiveness of church signage

GREETING UPON ARRIVAL: Rates the mystery guest's welcome by the official greeters or ushers

PRESERVICE ATMOSPHERE: Rates how the congregation or pastor interacts with the mystery guest and each other before the service begins

SEATING: Rates the seating options and arrangement

MUSIC: Rates the overall music of the service

IN-SERVICE GREETING: Rates the greeting by the congregation or pastor of the church during the service

MESSAGE: Rates the delivery of the main message. It does not address theology or whether the mystery guest agrees or disagrees with the content of the sermon.

SPEAKER: Rates the public speaking skills of the person leading the service including any video, props, images, and so on

POST-SERVICE ATMOSPHERE: Rates how the congregation or pastor interacts with the mystery guest and each other when the service is concluded

INFORMATION: Rates the availability, clarity, and thoroughness of the church's website, pamphlets, and other printed literature

FRIENDLINESS: Rates the friendliness of church

CHILDREN'S/YOUTH: Rates the overall impression of the children's ministry

DIVERSITY AND OUTREACH: Rates how diverse the church is and how it connects with its community with respect to age, socio-economic status, gender, and various ethnicities that live in the area.

RETURN: Mystery guests indicate whether or not they would return to this church for a second visit based on this initial experience

OVERALL EXPERIENCE: Mystery guests summarize the experience as a whole and may also provide suggestions or feedback on anything not covered by other categories

Consolidated Index Statistics from Faith Perceptions as of June 1, 2014

(includes numerical ratings for all churches measured to date)

4,288 unique mystery guest visits

450 churches included

Average weekly attendance per church is 310

59 percent of mystery guests are female; 41 percent are male

65 percent of services are traditional; 28 percent are contemporary; 7 percent are blended

96 percent of mystery guests believe in God or some higher power

24 percent of mystery guests do not identify with any formal denomination

22 percent of mystery guests were not raised with any formal denomination

80 percent of mystery guests are "unchurched" (meaning they don't have a church home)

Average age of mystery guests is thirty-nine and 76 percent are under fifty years old

Faith Perceptions hired individual, nonchurched guests to attend worship services of the congregations we were consulting in (twelve visits per church). When hired, a mystery worshipper attends worship (usually in the three months preceding the consultation). After attending, worshippers would complete a numeric rating and commentary. This information is sent to Faith Perceptions and compiled into a mystery worshipper report (usually over one hundred pages). This report is given to the consultation team prior to the consultation weekend.

Faith Perceptions created the following scoring index:

Lower than 6.5: very poor

6.5–7.0: poor

7.01–7.5: fair

7.51–8.0: good

Higher than 8.0: very good

The three areas of first impressions that rank lowest overall are community awareness, diversity and outreach, and return. These ranked in a "very poor" or "poor" ranking on a scale of 1–10.

Community Awareness: (rated 6.49) This consistently ranks as one of the lowest-rated categories because churches do a poor job of letting the community know they are there—especially to the unchurched population. Ineffective or missing signage, lack of traditional marketing, and "transactional" outreach (not having human contact; e.g., writing checks, donating food) are the primary culprits for low ratings. Often, signage is small, hard to see, poorly placed, or just not there at all. One of the first things to go (if it was ever there to begin with) is the marketing budget. That's unfortunate because, believe it or not, traditional marketing (done well) such as a direct mail is an effective way to introduce the church and invite people from the community. Nothing makes a greater impact and lets a community know who you are than *true* outreach efforts, but there is a big difference in "transactional" outreach and "missional" outreach (reaching people for Jesus Christ). "Missional" outreach bears fruit; the other does not.

Diversity and Outreach: (rated 6.05) Churches that don't truly reach out, connect, and build relationships with people through missional outreach aren't bringing in new faces or impacting the community the way they expect. The old saying, "People don't care how much you know until they know how much you care," applies here. Outreach that involves getting to know people by doing life with people (not just meeting a monetary need) are the building blocks for creating relationships with people of all ages and ethnicities (if ethnic diversity is relevant to the area). And because churches lack diversity (families, college age, children/youth), people do not see the church as reaching out to diversify nor do they want to stick around when there is not anyone their age or their child's age with whom to build community.

Return: (rated 6.86) The reasons people list for not wanting to come back to the church vary greatly, but they boil down to three things: (1) an unfriendly or unwelcoming church, (2) a mediocre worship experience, and (3) few people present in their age range or stage of life.

Worship has more passion, attachment, and history than most anything else in church. It is the identity of the congregation. There is emotion attached to it. There is attachment to style and time. If you are going to die on a hill, this is the hill to die on. But you have to be strategic in how you will go about this. For if you are not careful, you will have died on the hill and nothing will have changed, and this sets the church back for years. Nothing will get a pastor sent away from a church more quickly than messing with worship unsuccessfully. This is also a place where you can lose more people faster than through any other mistakes you can make. Yet this is the area that is in the most desperate need of improvement. We have seen churches try to make changes in worship without having any chips in the bank, which are earned through relationships within the congregation. It takes lots of chips to ask your folks to trade their preferences and likes for a different worship approach.

Hurt and pain around any attempts at changing worship styles, times, preference, and likes sometimes show up in consultations. Sometimes this is pain from the very distant past. Sometimes they show up in interviews with staff and key leaders. Other times, they may show up in the focus group. We hear a lot of conversation about differences in preferences for music genre than anything else. Most churches get stuck here because maintaining relationships with their fellow participants is deemed a higher priority over creating excellent, passionate worship contextualized to the mission field. Worship choices are made based on the time of worship just as much as style. Normally, the smaller the church, the harder it is to change worship times.

Here is an example of the time and style dilemma one church faced. A growing, competent, and compelling church has two traditional services. The sanctuary is half full at one service and one-third full at the other. This same church has a third service that is contemporary. The sanctuary at the contemporary service is overflowing. Now the church has stopped growing. To the outsider, it is obvious this church needs to go to two contemporary services and one traditional service to match the mission field. But when this very solution has been tried in the past, it blows up the church. The traditional service attenders will not change times.

Our church folks oftentimes don't appreciate, respect, or value other worship styles. They have trouble valuing a worship experience different from their own current worship experience. Worship attenders are often labeled by their worship time/style. Worshippers are sometimes even antagonistic and nasty towards each other when it comes to worship disagreements. Many times, they even make derogatory remarks.

Another symptom of a noncompelling worship experience is the low return rate of guests. If the church is having guests, but they are not returning for a second time, there is a disconnect somewhere. We must explore the reasons for this issue and resolve them. And it must be resolved quickly before the church gains a reputation as a noncompelling church.

Worship excellence is many times absent. Churches are sometimes just going through the motions of worship. They lack creativity and don't strive for excellence each and every Sunday. There is no evaluation process. Most times, there is no team approach in working toward creating excellent, contextually relevant worship experiences every week. Worship is sometimes performance based rather than based in spiritual gifts to create a passionate, excellent opportunity to praise and worship God. Worship is sometimes sloppy, slow, unrehearsed, or predictable with no attention to smooth and well-timed segues.

While hospitality is oftentimes written as a separate prescription, problems with hospitality many times show up during the worship experience. If hospitality were an issue for a particular church, it would become obvious from the mystery worshipper report. Along with hospitality, another key issue that may show up on Sunday morning is a lack of connection process (see chapter 6 for more on that).

Sometimes the worship issue is a timing issue. This could mean the time of day of the worship experience. It could also refer to the flow of the Sunday morning schedule. Sunday school, multiple worship experiences, children's options during worship, and fellowship/hospitality opportunities, to name a few, can all contribute to timing issues. I (Kay) was once leading a consultation weekend and encountered this full-blown timing issue. I arrived about twenty minutes prior to the worship start time. When I walked into the building, there was not a soul to be found. You see, Sunday school was still being held, so everyone was tied up in a class. There was no one available for hospitality. Sunday school was released only a few minutes before the start of worship. Imagine guests walking into this situation! They could have easily walked in, thought no one was around and left without anyone ever knowing they were there!

Other common issues found in the worship experience that need to be addressed are of a technical nature. These include use of multimedia, sound systems, lighting, signage, building presentation, restroom location and condition, nursery location and condition, and so on. All of these technical issues can affect the worship experience.

It is just really hard to get people motivated to help with hospitality if worship is bad. People are unlikely to invite guests because they are embarrassed about the worship experience their guest will receive. Churches can sometimes engage people in the mission field, but then can't offer a good worship experience when they finally get them into the sanctuary.

Let's go back to where we started this chapter. Worship is the fuel for the fire. You just have to get this right!

Prescriptions

Example One

On or before [date], the pastor, in consultation with the coach, will appoint a worship evaluation team to evaluate the current Sunday morning worship experience. The evaluation will include worship locations, music, ensembles, choirs, band, schedule, children's ministry, and technology needed to create an intellectually stimulating, emotionally moving, missionally relevant, and life-applicable worship experience for both the churched and unchurched. This team will visit and evaluate other churches where traditional and contemporary services are done with excellence. Visiting locations will be determined in consultation with the coach and pastor. The team will pay particular attention to media, sound, use of space, and integration of worship arts in a relevant worship service. When this report is accepted, the worship schedule will be changed to two services and implemented no later than [date].

Example Two

By [date], the pastor in consultation with the coach will appoint a worship evaluation team to evaluate the current worship experience. The evaluation will include music, ensembles, children's ministry, hospitality, and technology needed to create an intellectually stimulating, emotionally moving, missionally relevant, and life-applicable worship experience for both the churched and unchurched. This team will evaluate other churches where traditional services are done with excellence such as [church name and location]. The team will pay particular attention to media, sound, use of space, and integration of worship arts in a relevant traditional service. The [name of fund] will be made available to implement needed musical changes recommended by the worship evaluation team. An improved worship experience will be implemented by [date].

Example Three

In order to improve the worship experience, the pastor, in consultation with the leadership team chair and the lay leader, will appoint two teams. One team will represent the traditional worship service and the other will represent the contemporary worship service.

Each team will meet with the coach to evaluate and develop plans for improvement of the worship experience. The first meeting will be by [date]. Both teams will communicate with the leadership team and other ministry teams as they implement new plans. The implementation will begin over the summer of [year].

The teams will visit other churches for ideas to enhance the worship experiences. They will study the mystery worshipper report to understand experiences of new people attending our services. The improvements will address all areas of the services and must include, but are not limited to, the following:

⊕ Audio technology

⊕ Worship screen creativity and content

⊕ Flow, transitions, greeting, and order of services, including announcements and prayer time

⊕ Seating toward the front to overcome the feeling of disconnected, empty space

⊕ Music, including choir, praise band, instrumentals and vocals, variety of songs

Remedy

The starting point for most worship experience prescriptions is with the formation of a worship evaluation team. It is important for the leaders to first start with being brutally honest with one another about how worship is really going. If you believe your worship experience is good, hire mystery worshippers to either confirm or debunk your beliefs. Even in our very best worship experiences, there is always room for improvement. Trying to improve your worship is one of the most difficult changes for a church. It is packed with landmines, emotions, personalities, and attachments. If there is ever a time for coaching, it is coaching around worship. The team needs to first understand what the church is up against inside the congregation. Have a full understanding of what you are going to have to do inside the congregation to make some changes. The team also needs to understand what relevant, contextual worship is and then what it should look like in their mission field. They must also begin to understand the different worship options such as inspirational, educational, transformational, mission-connectional, caregiving, healing, or coaching.[2] They should learn, "It's not about attracting people into a 'church family'.... It's about blessing people who are strangers to grace."[3] Once the worship options are fully understood, the team must then determine which worship option best fits their mission field. This is where the team has to fully grasp their demographics both outside and inside the church. If the church desires to grow (and if it is living out its mission, it will desire this), then it must have those outside the church (those who don't have a relationship with Jesus Christ) as its primary mission field. This is the time for the team to pick up their demographics report, mystery worshipper report, and community study and review them carefully and extensively. For in this information the best option for worship will emerge.

Once the team is trained on contextual worship options, the team is then sent out to experience excellent, relevant, contextual, and compelling worship. The coach should be able to recommend churches that offer such an experience. These visits aren't for the team to learn what another church is doing and duplicate it. The purpose of the visits is to learn about and experience contextual, relevant, and compelling worship done with excellence. The team will be able to experience all aspects of the worship experience including hospitality, connection process, use of multimedia, being a part of an engaged congregation, a sermon delivered with excellence and context, great music, tight segues/transitions, great worship leading, and postworship discipleship opportunities. See the worship evaluation team's evaluation forms on the HCI website. *Worship Ways for the People Within Your Reach* by Thomas G. Bandy and Lucinda S. Holmes is a good resource for determining relevant worship for your particular context.[4]

Note: When I (Kay) coach a church with this prescription, I have the team travel together for their church visits, if at all possible. It is optimal to conduct all the visits in one weekend (i.e., one service on Saturday night and two on Sunday). I, too, like to travel along with the team. I am then able to coach them before and after. As a coach, you are able to continuously ask questions, call things to the team's attention, and help keep the team focused. It also creates opportunities to work while we travel. The team can do a lot of processing on such things as what they saw, what they experienced, what they learned, and what they are

---

2. These worship options are detailed in Thomas G. Bandy and Lucinda S. Holmes, *Worship Ways for the People Within Your Reach* (Nashville: Abingdon Press, 2014).

3. Lucinda S. Holmes, "It's Not about the Coffee: Mission Targeted Worship," presentation, June 9, 2014, http://www.slideshare.net/RevLsh/its-not-about-the-coffee-mission-targeted-worship.

4. Bandy and Holmes, *Worship Ways*.

taking away from the experience for application back home. The team will also be capturing information about their visits on the evaluation forms. When the team travels together, they have the opportunity to arrive early and drive around the mission field of the church so they can fully understand the context in which the church is working. This team weekend experience can be very insightful and a shifting experience for many team members. This might be the first time they have experienced another worship service outside their home church. It might also be the first time they have experienced excellent worship or radical hospitality or have looked at worship through the eyes of the mission field rather than their own worship preferences.

Once the team has finished the church visits and completed the evaluation forms, the team gathers together to share how the churches they visited demonstrated excellent, contextually relevant, and compelling worship for that particular mission field. Once the team can connect how other churches do this, it is much easier for them to and more likely that they will implement changes in their own church and mission field. After the team debriefs, they then begin to process how to create an excellent, contextually relevant, and compelling worship experience for their own mission field. If the list of recommendations for changes, transitions, shifts, and new additions to worship is too long, the team may need to create priority lists for their leadership team's consideration. For example, there may be items to complete in the next ninety days, then six months, and then next year. Don't let this team get caught up in "how" to implement. Their task is to develop a report outlining what is needed to take the church to the next level (or two) of excellent, contextually relevant, and compelling worship experiences. This report is then handed off to the leadership team, and the work of the worship evaluation team is complete.

The recommendations outlined in the report from the worship evaluation team are handed off to a worship design team for implementation. This team might be newly developed, preexisting, or working on completing some of the tasks but in need of training in order to shift to a fully functioning worship design team.

The worship design team is an eclectic group of individuals with a diverse set of gifts, skills, passions, and talents to create and bring together an excellent, contextually relevant, and compelling worship experience each and every Sunday. The pastor will either present to the team or collaborate with the team on sermon series topics and scriptures. The task of the worship design team is to collaborate together to bring all the different worship elements into a cohesive, excellent worship experience. These elements include song selection (before, during, and after the worship service), video clips, prayers, drama, dance, digital pictures, visual effects for the altar and chancel area, bulletin design or notes, congregational handouts (e.g., paper, notecards, rocks, crosses), lighting effects, segues, and readings, to name a few.

For best results, the worship design team is working three to six months out. This gives plenty of opportunity for individual team member research and team collaboration. Many teams have found it to be beneficial to do semiannual retreats for the purposes of long-term worship planning. They then meet more frequently to work out more of the details.

In addition to working together on planning worship, the team also evaluates worship. The sooner after the conclusion of worship, the better for effective evaluation. Some worship design teams meet for ten minutes after worship and share evaluation on three major questions:

1. What went well?

2. What didn't make the mark?

3. What would we do differently?

If an evaluation conversation immediately following worship is not conducive for the team and pastor, then a Monday morning gathering could be an option. Some teams send out a Sunday afternoon e-mail with a recap of the answers to the previous questions. If you get much past Monday afternoon, not only do people's memories begin to fade, but also the team gets busy with life and it just won't happen. Weekly evaluation is critical for learning from experiences and making sure we are doing what we planned. Weekly evaluation is also critical to keeping the bar of excellence before us and continuing to raise it.

When assembling the worship design team, the pastor should be looking for a collection of the following qualities:

○ Creativity

○ Collaborative work style (plays off others without being too shy but isn't too take-charge)

○ Team player who also follows through on individual work

○ An eye for detail

○ Ability to see the big picture

○ Aptitude for visual effects (props, images, design, and so on)

○ Technically savvy

○ Millennial

○ Musically talented

○ Spiritual depth

Case Studies

Case Study One

First United Methodist Church of West Plains went through the HCI experience. One of our prescriptions was to change the time of worship at our early service from 8:15 a.m. to 9:00 a.m. This change would cause the elimination of a popular, fifteen-minute refreshment time in between the early service and Sunday school, which starts at 10:00 a.m. But we went ahead and implemented the change and saw a dramatic increase in worship attendance. It wasn't so much that we attracted new people to the later time start, but most of our younger families had an easier time getting to worship at 9:00 a.m. rather than 8:15 a.m. So we saw an increase in more regular attendance. We have had to shorten Sunday school, but we seem to be managing that sufficiently. We provide coffee and donuts before the early service and for people to grab on their way out of worship to Sunday school. The growth in our early service has forced us to consider ways to accommodate the need for extra seating. —Mark Mildren, senior pastor of First UMC in West Plains, MO

Case Study Two

The worship experience has changed drastically from when the HCI process began. The pastor and the worship staff and servant volunteers have endeavored over the past four years to evaluate each worship experience with the goal of reaching people being introduced to Jesus Christ primarily, while also offering depth during worship. Music and preaching have improved overall and hopefully will continue to improve. Through study of our ministry context (using MissionInsite) and through experience, Community UMC made the bold decision to take two "blended" worship services on Sunday morning and make the early service a traditional service (Traditions) and the later service a more indigenous contemporary-type service (Catalyst). We are still assessing the success of these worship services, although we've seen a 30 percent growth in our "Traditions" worship service and a 20 percent increase in first-time visitors to our "Catalyst" service. I appreciate what Bishop Schnase shared with me late last year when he was a guest preacher at Community—"Hey, you've really stepped it up in your music here." We are always evaluating our worship experiences with the mission to make new disciples for Jesus Christ in mind. —Kevin Shelton, pastor of Community UMC in Columbia, MO

Case Study Three

We had a prescription related to our most recently formed worship service. Basically we were challenged to bring it up to a level of excellence that would be attractive to unchurched and de-churched folks. The prescription called for realignment of a staff position, intentional upgrading of music and vocal quality, drastic overhaul of the worship environment, and immediate front-burner attention given to radical hospitality, both in personnel and resources. This was not an easy path and was not without considerable pushback. Some people in our more long-term worship services were uneasy with the time and attention given to our newest service. And people who were a part of the service receiving the most prescription treatment resisted some of the needed changes. However, because of this prescription, overall worship attendance has gone from a low of 310 in 2009 to nearly 600 now. More important than that, the overwhelming majority of new commitments to Jesus Christ and baptisms happen in the service that was the primary target of the prescription. —Geoff Posegate, lead pastor of First UMC in Sikeston, MO

Case Study Four

The prescriptions that have had the most impact and fruit are really two prescriptions working together. (1) Adding a praise worship service and (2) Small groups for intentional faith development. As a result of implementing these prescriptions there has been an increase of 10 percent in worship attendance, while the number of small groups have gone from four to thirteen and our youth program is up from twenty-five to sixty. The greatest growth is not in numbers but in spirituality of the congregation. The fruit of the spiritual growth, I believe, is the hunger for serving God and gathering together to discover next steps in the life of Harper Chapel UMC.

To accomplish the growth, Harper Chapel went through some growing pains as we changed service times, added to the financial budget, and worked through the scheduling of building usage. There had to be much planning and open conversation to accommodate the growth. When we added the praise service, we also moved the time of the traditional service. In that process we only lost two families, or a total of four people, while gaining three families that were able to come

43

back due to the service times. With all this being said, I believe that greatest fruit of all is that Harper Chapel now has a new focus on our mission and purpose of making disciples of Jesus Christ and are transforming the lake area and the world. —Jon Thompson, pastor of Harper Chapel UMC in Osage Beach, MO

Summary

	Compelling	Noncompelling
Leadership	Always evaluating, improving, time priority	It's okay...no attention, just how it's always been
Congregation	Inspiring, motivating, don't want to miss	Don't want to bring friends, makes excuses for its shortcomings
Community	Known for the music or preachingy	Nonexistent

Group Questions

1. Has the leadership of your church ever truly evaluated your worship?

2. How would you honestly describe your current worship experience?

3. What obstacles would you incur that would stop you from making improvements to your worship?

4. Share a time when you have experienced uninspiring worship.

5. Share a time when you have experienced great worship.

Chapter Four
Community Connection

Prevailing Symptoms

In the Saturday workshop during an HCI consultation weekend, we start out by asking how the participants came to be a part of their church. More than 75 percent of the responses indicate that members were either born into the church, grew up in the church, or married into the families of that church. It has become very obvious to us that The United Methodist Church (and we suspect other mainline churches) is a very family and generationally oriented church. Very few people walk into our doors from the community who don't already have a connection to the families of the church. Once in a while we might run into a new suburban church where there was an invitational culture in the 1980s or 1990s that attracted people beyond their generation and family. However, this is a small minority.

In almost all of our churches that are stagnate or declining, there is a significant gap between who the church is and who is in the community. Most of the churches we worked with thought they looked like and represented the community. They thought the community looked like them. But, in fact, we have found that our churches are thirty to forty years older than the community they are in, and far less diverse. Over the years, a significant number of churches that began as neighborhood congregations have become drive-in congregations, meaning that people used to live in the neighborhood but since have moved out of the community. But, because of their loyalties to the congregation, they continue to drive back to the building in the old neighborhood. The church most likely made an intentional decision a decade or two earlier for their church to stay in this community. Then, over the ensuing decade, the church actually moved. The building stayed. But if the church is the people, then the church actually moved and now drives back to the community on Sunday morning still believing that

45

they are just as connected to the community as they were ten years ago and that nothing has changed. We also find a disconnect when church folks think they know their community based on their experiences with their peers. What we find is that many church folks hang out with other church folks. We are not very interactive with unchurched people in our communities, so we base all of our thoughts, feelings, and ideas about the communities based on our own circle of churched influences.

Whatever way it has happened, most churches have become disconnected to the community that surrounds them. It doesn't matter if they are rural, county seat, suburban, or central city churches. We, as churches, are very isolated. We are like islands unto ourselves most of the time. We dispatch acts of good deeds out into the community. We write checks to social agencies to help people in our communities. But we rarely make personal connections with the unchurched in our communities.

Another question we frequently ask during a consultation weekend is, "Would anybody notice if your church were to close tomorrow?" Would anyone in your community notice, other than those already connected to the church? It has been sort of puzzling to me (Bob) that as a judicatory leader, I have never received a call from a community leader asking me why we have closed the local United Methodist Church in their community. More than eighty churches have closed in Missouri in the past eight years. Yet no one called to ask where the United Methodist churches went! It is an obvious sign to me that we were not very impactful in those communities. Most of the time, this is a surprise to congregations, and they become defensive about it. Congregations recite a list of events they host or contributions that they make to other agencies to help in the communities. Sometimes they will list people from the congregation doing great community service. But when asked if the community would know if they were doing this on behalf of the church, the answer is mostly no.

One of the methods we use to address this community connection issue is to perform a ministry audit. First, we start with an exhaustive list of each and every activity the church conducts (worship, Sunday school, Scouts, potlucks, fundraisers, and so on). If you were to categorize each of the events in the life of your church, which category would they fall in? Is the event for us (fellowship, entertain, edify)? Is the event teaching (disciple, equip, evangelize)? Is the event to serve the community in mission work (external and equipping/evangelism)? Is the event to reach new people (evangelism)? Is the activity for those inside the church or outside the church (internal or external)? Is it for the community and mission (evangelism)? A healthy church has a mixture of events in each box of the diagram below. Where do the activities of your church fall within these boxes? Is

FOCUS

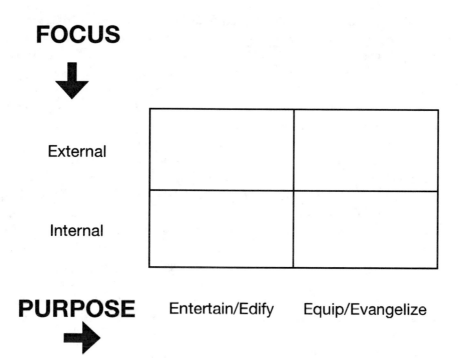

External

Internal

PURPOSE   Entertain/Edify   Equip/Evangelize

it a healthy mix? Is there an emphasis in one particular box? What did you learn from this exercise?

We found that most church events are fellowship based. In other words, they are for us churched folks. That is, the focus is on enjoying the company of our church family. We have come to know and expect this as primary function of the church. These events might be disguised under other titles, but the bottom line is that they create the opportunity to hang out with our church friends and family. Over time we begin to believe that fellowship is the primary function of our church. We seem to forget that the mission of the church is to make new disciples of Jesus Christ for the transformation of the world. Some people even get offended by the suggestion to take an existing event and invite new people! Some people have gotten offended by the proposal to imagine offering a particular event as an evangelism opportunity. The mission of Jesus Christ is difficult to accomplish when we primarily hang out with people who already have a relationship with Jesus Christ. The biggest danger we all run into as Christians is to hang out only with other Christians and not reach beyond our circle of influence, friends, and family.

We also sometimes categorize an event as outreach/evangelism when it is truly a fundraiser. We may call it a community dinner to fund missions. We "open it up" to the community by putting a sign advertising it in the front lawn of the church. If an unchurched person from the community would happen to drop in for the dinner, we would ask them to pay for dinner or at least we would put the basket out for a "love offering." We don't practice radical hospitality, get their names, or sit with them as they enjoy our delicious United Methodist cooking. No, what we really did, in essence, is ask them to fund the ministry to reach them or people like them. Really! We ask the very people we are trying to reach to fund the ministry to reach them! It is crazy!

Many churches believe having an evangelism committee/team suffices. In other words, the congregation delegates the responsibility of sharing the good news with people to a committee, thus giving the individual congregants either an excuse not to do it or the privilege and honor of participating. We certainly need a team of people organizing evangelism efforts, but the team needs to be focusing on equipping the congregation for evangelism—not just doing all the work themselves. Other times, churches see evangelism as reconnecting with people who have fallen away from the church. Outwardly focused, healthy congregations see evangelism as building relationships with the unchurched so that they might have a relationship with Jesus Christ. While the pastor should be a model for an evangelist, we all have responsibility for being evangelists. Congregants can't get off the hook for evangelizing by saying it is the pastor's job. We are *all* called to share the good news!

It is important to reacquaint yourself with your mission field. Once we have clearly realized and identified the size of the gap in our perceptions of the community and the reality of the community, it is important to understand your mission field. Before you start down the journey of church transformation, be sure you know your mission field. Don't just think you know your mission field. Know for certain that you know your mission field. First, collect the data. We in the Missouri Annual Conference use MissionInsite for this purpose. Second, immerse yourself in the mission field to confirm the data. Many times a congregation thinks they know their mission field, but often they are mistaken. Their understanding of the mission field is based on their personal associations, which are usually other churched people. With nearly 80 percent of the population of America unchurched, we churched people don't always have a good grip on the reality of the demographics in our mission field. First caution: Make sure you are looking at your immediate neighborhood. Sometimes heavier populated areas have a smaller mission field (e.g., one-mile radius) while more rural churches have larger mission fields (e.g., five-mile radius). Second caution: You must first relationally reconnect with your mission field. An invitation is empty without first building a relationship and trust. The church is not a valued entity in communities today. We have to reestablish our value in the community before we invite new people to come.

If mission and vision is critical, if hospitality is paramount to be a healthy church, connecting to your mission field is just as important. There is no need proceeding to any of the other chapters if you don't do this.

The days of "if you build it, they will come" are over. The days of "just get the right program going and they will come" are over. The days of "you come to us" are over. We must move to a culture of "we go to you." This is not remedied quickly. It could take months or sometimes even years to accomplish. This is yet another culture change in our church that must be made in order for our church to be compelling in the years to come.

Prescriptions

Example One

On or before [date], the pastor, in consultation with the coach, will assemble a community connection team of four to six people. The purpose of the team is to oversee the planning, execution, and follow-up on one service blitz (a day of good deeds in the neighborhood) and two bridge events (sole purpose to build relationships with people in the neighborhood). One of the two bridge events will be held offsite. All three events will be conducted no later than [date] and will be "all church" events. The coach will equip and train the team for these events.

Example Two

The pastor, in consultation with the coach, will work with the existing mission team to facilitate an "intentional community connection" effort. This team will begin to lay out the following activities of the church for [year] and [year] by [date]:

1. Research and act upon the "felt" needs of people in your community and opportunities for services through interviews with local officials, police chief, fire chief, council members, local public health department, school superintendents and principals, and two neighborhood focus groups on or before [date].

2. Conduct at least two community events (at no charge to the public and not specifically for your members) to reach new people and build relationships twice a year beginning on [date]. At least one of these events is to be held off the church grounds.

3. Conduct at least two service events to share the love of God with the community twice a year beginning on [date]. At least one of these events is to be held off the church grounds.

4. Plan and facilitate these events and then continue for a second year in [year] to continue to evaluate and plan events and activities that will help connect the church with the community.

Remedy

The coach will train the community connection or bridge team. The team's job is to plan the event, recruit, and train the congregation to execute the event and then create and implement a follow-up process. The team shouldn't be the only ones executing—these events must be seen as "all hands on deck" in order to fully execute them with excellence.

The bridge events should be held outside the church and preferably offsite. We need to remove as many barriers as possible for the unchurched. Sometimes the actual church facility itself is a barrier for folks. By going to the people rather than having the expectation for them to come to us, we remove a possible barrier. Other barriers we need to remove to be able to build relationships with those in our community include no preaching, no prayers, no pocketbooks, and no pressure. We refer to this as providing a "P-Free" zone for bridge events. We want to provide the opportunity for the unchurched to see us churched folks as just regular folks like them. After we have the opportunity over time to build an authentic relationship, we can share our story and our church. But, we must first offer ourselves for a relationship with them in a nonthreatening method and environment to build trust.

In order to plan a contextually relevant and therefore well-attended (by the unchurched in the community) event, the bridge team must study their mission field's demographics. What are the needs of the community and how might the church plug into meeting those needs? What activities does the community enjoy participating in? What are missing services in the community? The event should be planned to meet the needs of the community, not the congregation. Remember, bridge events have the sole purpose of building relationships with the unchurched in your mission field. Also remember that radical hospitality is crucial for these events. Don't put all the church people to work "doing" things; open your hospitality team up to their primary task of being with the people, making them feel welcome, having conversations, giving directions, and so on.

The church will need a prayer team for the bridge events. This team will pray for the bridge team, the mission field, the pastor, and the forthcoming attendees.

They will pray over the space before the event. They will silently walk the space and continue to pray for the attendees, community, bridge team, and pastor. The prayer team will continue to pray after the event for those following up with the attendees and building relationships.

At each bridge event, there needs to be a method to collect names. Remember, the sole purpose of bridge events is to build relationships with the unchurched. It is difficult to build relationships if we don't have names and contact information. This is usually accomplished by having some sort of drawing. Tie in the drawing to the event and demographics. For example, if you are doing a family-focused event, have a drawing for four tickets to attend the circus coming to town next month. If the event is focused on those economically challenged, you might offer a gift certificate to the local grocery store. Sometimes local merchants will even donate merchandise or gift certificates in exchange for the advertising at the event.

Once the event is over, divide the names collected among the people who will be following up and building relationships. This team should be recruited and in place during the planning stages of the event. Do not wait until the event is over to figure out your follow-up process! The follow-up is critical and must be timely. If you don't have a follow-up system and plans to implement it, don't have the event! If you are not fully committed to the follow-up, then you are not ready to hold the event. Your church has not yet turned the corner on the community connection as their priority. Those following up will be praying for their names. They will drop a handwritten note in the mail within two or three days of the event thanking them for attending and introducing themselves. Another note will follow in a week or two asking if there is anything they or the church can do to be helpful. In another week or two, send another note. Then make a phone call asking if there is anything they or the church can do to be helpful. Only after there is a connection/relationships, do they ask if the person has a church home where they regularly attend. If not, invite them to be your guest at either an event or worship.

Plan for handoffs. In other words, always plan a next step for your guests. So after they attend a block party, what is a possible next step for them? Have that planned and available to talk about. Worship cannot be the only handoff. Going from a bridge event straight to worship is sometimes too big of a leap for an unchurched person. What is another possible step that is less intimidating for them? Perhaps it is some sort of class on parenting, budgeting, or cooking. We also need to have a guest-friendly or guest-focused sermon series that follows bridge events. The sermon series would meet the needs of our guests. A popular topic for a sermon series following bridge events centers on relationships (e.g., parenting, romance, marriage).

So many times we church people mistake good deeds as being the end-all of our church responsibility. We good church people give of our time to serve on communities. We well-meaning church people give of our resources to write checks to fund good causes in our community. We well-meaning church people go out into our community and do service projects to benefit others both as a church and individually. Yet, many times we get caught up in believing that is all that is asked of us as Christians. May we offer up something to consider?

What if, instead of adding a couple of extra cans of green beans to our grocery cart, which is in turn then piled onto the altar and celebrated and forgotten, we do something different? What if instead we connect with the recipient of that much-needed can of green beans? Rather than the cans being transferred to a food bank, the recipient could come to know us. We could come to know them. We could let them know why we choose to feed the hungry and how we are blessed to be able to do so. We could let them know why we choose to believe in our God. We could let them know that Christ loves us and loves them unconditionally. We could offer the grace of Christ.

Rather than donating a coat to a local charity, why don't we find a way to connect with the person needing the coat so that we could offer not only a good deed but also the good news? For combining the good deed with the good news is what God calls us to do. We seem to stop with only the good deeds! Bridge events give us the opportunity to do both! We can offer many reasons for why it happens, but now that we understand our responsibility and, more importantly, our privilege, it is time to offer both the good deeds and the good news to the unchurched in our mission field.

Case Study

After much prayer and conversation within our church, we made the decision to begin trying some new things in and for our community. We decided as a church to hold a "Back to School Bash." The "Back to School Bash" would be held on the Saturday before school started. We would partner with Ozark Area Community Action Corporation (OACAC) to provide backpacks, school supplies, and new shoes to area children whose families might not be able to afford these items. We also talked about grilling hot dogs and providing a free lunch to those who attended.

After much conversation, I brought up the idea of asking First Baptist Church (FBC) to join us in this mission project. Our two churches are located right next to each other and FBC has a large Family Life Center that we could use for the event. I talked with their pastor, and he was right on board with all our plans. He and I also thought it would be a great way for all the churches in Cassville to get united around a wonderful mission project and show our community that we, as Christ followers, are not into bickering with one another but join together to share the love of Jesus with our community. And so for the past two years on the Saturday before school starts, we have held the "Back to School Bash" on the campuses of our church and First Baptist Church. The first year, 2012, we served probably around 150 children. This past year we were able to assist around four hundred children not only in Cassville but also in other Barry County communities.

I believe that because of this outreach project, as well as another project called "Kindness in Action," we, as Cassville UMC, have seen an increase in young families getting involved in the life of the church. This past year, 2013, we have received into membership sixteen new people all by profession of faith, with a vast majority being young adults. I have been told by the young adults in our church that getting out in our community and helping those who are in need of help is very important to them and a major reason they are attending and joining our church. I have also heard that several of the other churches in Cassville have seen an increase in attendance. All because our churches are unified in working together to show the love and grace of God through outreach and mission projects. —Andy Lambel, pastor of Cassville UMC in Cassville, MO

Summary

	Compelling	Noncompelling
Leadership	Understand their mission field	Significant gap between congregation and mission field
Congregation	Engaged hands-on in mission field	Hosting inward events and writing checks to social agencies
Community	Trusted, feeling the impact of the church	Disconnected, not known or trusted

Group Questions

1. Has your church identified your targeted mission field?

2. Have you studied the demographic information for the targeted mission field?

3. Have you taken a prayer walk through your mission field?

4. Are you a hands-on engaged church in the mission field or is your church just writing checks?

5. Share a time when you were engaged hands-on in your targeted mission field on behalf of the church.

Intentional Faith
Development

Prevailing Symptoms

How does someone in your church go from being new to being an authentic follower of Jesus Christ? In the eight years of HCI, this may be the most puzzling question we ask. We get really fuzzy answers to this question. We often hear people say, "That is what Sunday school is for, right?" We often hear people say newcomers attend worship or a committee meeting. We have come to believe that if we come to worship, attend Sunday school, serve on a couple of committees, and participate in Vacation Bible School that somehow we become disciples. We have come to believe this happens by osmosis. If a consultation team discovers any faith development process, it is heavily curriculum based. If we just take the required classes or read the following materials, we are then mature disciples.

It became apparent to me (Bob) that my church just didn't have an intentional faith development process. I never put one together in any church I pastored, but after eight years of consulting in churches, I recognized that apparently we did have a bit of a faith development plan in those churches. But, it was unintentional rather than intentional. At best, the "plan" looked something like this:

○ Attend worship

○ Attend adult Sunday school

○ Send kids to Sunday school and Vacation Bible School

○ Send youth to youth group

○ Volunteer for a committee

○ Volunteer to help

○ Participate in a Bible study (women's, men's, or a topical group study)

The unintentional faith development process in churches I (Bob) led started in worship. From worship, you would either volunteer in ministry inside the church (e.g., hospitality or teaching) or ministry outside the church (service). Once a person was involved in ministry, he would be invited to a membership class and then into a growth group of some kind. There was nothing intentional about what went into those growth groups. From here, some people were asked to be leaders. But mostly people fell into the cracks. There was obviously a discipleship cliff. We rarely knew what happened to people because we were not tracking people very well. During staff meetings, my staff and I would wake up and ask, "Where are the Smiths? We haven't seen them lately." Of course, by then, it was too late. We missed the opportunity to first create and then to implement an intentional faith development process to grow disciples in these growth groups. Quite ironic, isn't it? By not discipling folks, we never taught them how to share their faith within their group, then in worship, so that they were then comfortable sharing their faith in their community. We missed teaching evangelism so we missed creating the multiplication opportunity for the kingdom.

In a newer church, they may be more aggressive and ask newer attendees to attend a membership class to convince them to attend their church rather than another church, with maybe a little bit of doctrine thrown in. Our unintentional faith development plan was that if you came to the church and hung around a bit, you would develop into an authentic follower of Jesus Christ. So how has that been working for us?

Churches think they are being productive if they have something going on in every room of the church on every night of the week. We (Bob and Kay) both sit here as a product of this process and have met thousands of others who are also products of this process. But it is the exception rather than the rule that somebody sort of "got it" about Jesus. This process produced people who worked really hard operating the church. It added a lot of busyness to a lot of already busy lives. And we have mistaken busyness as discipleship. We assumed if we took our kids to the building, the church would give them religion. Moderns (modern church leaders) believe that "spiritual health results from a largely private effort."[1] Most spiritual work really happens with both corporate and individual development. Here are the two ships passing in the night. Lay people and clergy, who were formed in the modern church era of expectations, believe that if they bring people to the church building they will get religious. Otherwise, the spiritual things are left to private effort. However, must of us didn't do the private, spiritual work. The clergy and lay leadership at the church formed in the modern era thought that the majority of the congregation would practice their spiritual pursuit at home in private. The church was mostly for fellowship and missions. Meanwhile, the congregants brought their children and youth to church thinking they would get their spiritual nourishment at the church. The results are hollowness, emptiness, and a group of people who know how to operate a church but seem a bit mystified when asked the question of their faith journey. We have a religious-based background rather than a spiritually based life.

During the consultation process, we interview leaders. Our conversation starts with asking them to tell us about their spiritual journeys. While this question was first formed to allow people to relax a bit and talk about themselves, it also revealed some very curious findings. When people were asked to share their faith story or journey, the majority of people actually talked to us about their church membership history. A church membership history would give details as to when they came to the church, how long they have been a member, what committees they have served on, and what Sunday school class they attend. People have a difficult time telling us about their personal relationship with Jesus Christ. If they do have a God moment to share, it is many times a story from twenty or more years ago. We have trouble seeing and recognizing God in everyday life. If we can't see God at work in our own daily lives, how can we share that with others—especially with others we don't know?

Most churches we encounter have an unintentional faith development process. At best, it leads people to church membership rather than discipleship (let alone becoming a mature believer who would share the good news with people they don't know). Churches that lack intentional faith development have no intentional process of helping folks move from guests to regular attenders to growing in their faith to mature believers who are sharing the good news with others. It is a rare church that understands and has puzzled through what the end result might look like in this intentional faith development process. Many times, leaders in our churches simply pick a book with an interesting book title in the bookstore or online and share it with their class or small group. There is no intentional thought on how that might connect someone to a pathway or how

---

1. Bob Whitesel, *Organix: Signs of Leadership in a Changing Church* (Nashville: Abingdon Press, 2011), 39.

it connects with other classes and ministries in the church. Because no one has ever thought this through, there is no set of character traits, beliefs, daily rituals, behaviors, or expectations outlined or taught in our local churches. In fact, we are not even sure that we should be describing an outcome. This gets even further complicated by some thinking that we shouldn't even have a prescribed outcome. One step further, there is not a ready-made clean set of instructions in the Bible for becoming followers of Jesus Christ. There are many lists included in the Bible: fruit of the Spirit (Gal 5:22-23), spiritual gifts (1 Cor 12:1-12, 27-31), and Paul's set of marks of a mature disciple (Eph 4:20-32). So the uncertainty has led us to do nothing. That hasn't worked so well.

Consequently, we have a shortage of discipleship. We have people who have been with us for a very long time, but their faith isn't necessarily any deeper than when they were confirmed. They are good, moral, nice people, but not necessarily disciples of Jesus Christ. Believing in God does not necessarily make you a follower of Jesus Christ. There is probably not a time when we have questioned the existence of God, but we have sometimes fallen off our discipleship. One of John Wesley's deepest fears was that we would have an outer form of religion with no inner substance. Our fear in the twenty-first century is that Wesley's fear is a reality for a great deal of us.

All of this has resulted in a church full of consumers. When you have an outward form of faith but lack inner substance of faith, you become easily upset when the leadership of the church begins to change the outward forms of that faith. When leaders change things around the building that signify the outer forms of faith, those with outward faith become very upset. For instance, if a person gave a picture of Jesus to the church that had a significant religious meaning attached to it for that person and then the church leadership wanted to later take the picture down, that person could become upset because the leaders removed one of their outward forms of spirituality. It is like removing that person's spirituality. It is the outward sign and symbol of a time when he or she felt close to God. Others have had that same experience simply with the moving of the baptismal font where their child was baptized. That baptismal font is related to a religious experience. Moving it is like trying to move the memory of being close to God. When our religious experiences are tied in things rather than our relationship with Christ (our God moments) we are missing the connection of the maturity and substance of our faith. This is part of our disease. We have an outer form, but lack an inner substance of our faith. When we had a church-centered culture where religious symbols meant a lot to the whole culture, it was easier to simply have an outer form of faith without any inner substance. Now that our culture no longer values those same religious symbols, it is very difficult for folks not having an inner substance to not feel intimidated by the insistence of new leaders asking them to engage this strange culture when they themselves are struggling with the lack of an inner depth of faith. The stuff (our outer markers) became our connection, foundation, and understanding of Jesus Christ. If we had done a good job of helping people build a substance of faith rather than a religion and outward symbols, we might not be in this rapid state of decline. It is almost like we are back in biblical days when we had to build the very foundations of what it means to be faithful and fruitful as a follower of Jesus Christ.

So when you are talking about those difficult worship changes in chapter 3, like changing times, changing the building, and changing the music, understand that these are our outward substances of faith and this is why it is so difficult to change. This is a deeply spiritual problem.

Lack of an intentional faith development process many times also shows up as a lack of evangelism and generosity. Reverend Kendall Waller often says, "You can't give away something that you don't have." It is no wonder why when we ask people to share their faith with people they don't know, they are reluctant because they don't have a deep inner faith themselves. This is not their fault. They are good people. The system has produced what it is designed to produce. We are designed to produce members and that is what we have produced rather than disciples. What we are attempting to offer here is a process to develop discipleship rather than church membership. This may be why we are experiencing a lot of dropouts, mostly baby boomers who stayed with the church since they were kids. They have raised their kids, sent them off to college, and have left the church, feeling burnt out and empty inside. They have completed the tasks or checklist we have taught them to complete.

How can we expect people to grow in their faith if we don't have an intentional process/journey for them to do so? If we aren't developing their faith, how can we expect them to share the good news and look toward making new disciples? This is why Doug Anderson teaches a process on how to share our faith in *Get Their Name: Grow Your Church by Building New Relationships.*[2] They must first experience servant evangelism, then learn to share in a small group, and then share in worship before they are ready to share their faith in the mission field. We have to offer a process that leads them to be comfortable with sharing their faith.

Prescriptions

Example One

The pastor in consultation with the coach will assemble an intentional faith development team to ensure persons connected with [church name] have

---

2. Bob Farr, Doug Anderson, and Kay Kotan, *Get Their Name: Grow Your Church by Building New Relationships* (Nashville: Abingdon, 2013).

opportunities to grow on their spiritual journey, moving from guests to missionaries. The team will be charged with researching other churches' discipleship pathways as well as using *Deepening Your Effectiveness* as a resource in developing the pathway.[3] The pathway will be completed and rolled out to the church on or before [date].

Example Two

The pastor, in consultation with the coach, will put together a team of three people by [date] to create a clear discipleship path for moving people from where they are on their spiritual journey to becoming fully devoted followers of Jesus Christ. The team will discern a faith development plan within a Wesleyan model such as *The Race to Reach Out* by Doug Anderson or Church of the Resurrection's "Journey 101."[4] This plan will be put into place by [date]. The team and pastor will discern the practices of an authentic follower of Jesus Christ using Bishop Robert Schnase's book *Five Practices of Fruitful Living*.[5]

Example Three

A discipleship team of three to four people (one under age forty) will be assembled by the pastor, in consultation with the coach, on or before [date] to ensure persons connected with [church name] have opportunities to grow on their spiritual journey, moving from guest to missionary. The team will be charged with researching other churches' discipleship pathways as well as using *Deepening Your Effectiveness* as a resource in developing the pathway.[6] The pathway will be completed and rolled out to the church by [date].

Remedy

The very first myth we must debunk is that an intentional faith development process is creating a list of required curriculum. The journey of faith development is not curriculum identification. Rather it is how to grow more Christlike. What are the traits, beliefs, and experiences that your church desires people to have in order to grow in their faith and live it out daily? What would you want your people to know and experience so that their daily lives are changed to walk

---

3. Dan Glover and Claudia Levy, *Deepening Your Effectiveness* (Nashville: Discipleship Resources, 2006).

4. Doug Anderson, *The Race to Reach Out: Connecting Newcomers to Christ in a New Century* (Nashville: Abingdon Press, 2004).

5. Robert Schnase, *Five Practices of Fruitful Living* (Nashville: Abingdon Press, 2010).

6. Glover and Levy, *Deepening Your Effectiveness*.

closer to Christ? One of the ways to get to this question is to start with the end in mind. If you were to take a forty-year attender of your church and suck out all the faith, knowledge, and experience they have with a vacuum cleaner, what would you hope they would have gotten?

As stated before, there is no one, perfect clear-cut discipleship path to pull off a shelf or out of the Bible. Your pastor and leaders must work through for themselves what they think an authentic follower of Jesus Christ would look like. It may not be perfect, and it may change over time. But if you haven't designed a target to hit, you won't hit anything. This is why Bishop Schnase wrote the book *Five Practices of Fruitful Living*, as an attempt to give some markers for an authentic follower of Jesus Christ. Rick Warren did this also with *The Purpose Driven Life*.[7] These were both intended to help us figure out the target. Whether we agree with them or not, it was a great step and both books have sold thousands of copies. Warren's book has sold more than sixty million copies. There was an obvious hunger for such a resource.

Because our spiritual growth doesn't always move in a successive manner, our faith development pathway can't either. The pathway is never ending. We will never fully finish our spiritual work, thus the spiritual growth pathway will have no ending point either. The pathway is not sequential. We sometimes must rediscover a spiritual discipline, go deeper, or see in a new context where we are in our own spiritual journey. The pathway isn't a checklist. It is a pathway for spiritual growth and maturity. It is simply a map or guide that allows us to grow deeper in our faith and become more Christlike. You do need a map. It isn't as important to figure out the perfect steps as much as having and knowing the next step to take. The pathway might speak to the three types of grace: prevenient (preparing) grace, accepting (justifying) grace, and sustaining (sanctifying) grace. The process is not linear, and we could be in two places at the same time. We can backslide in our spiritual growth. Life happens! Wesley's understanding of grace looks linear, but it is not. Our churches need a map for faith development just as Wesley created a map of the elements of grace. This is why John Wesley refers to the Christian life as a way of life. It is not an exact science, but it is a life of practices. Therefore, you need to know the practices in order to live that way of life.

A discipleship or faith development team needs to be assembled to complete the work of creating the faith development pathway or process. The coach then conducts training with the team. The first order of business is defining an intentional faith development process. Those who have been attending Sunday school for years may have a difficult time grasping this. In coaching a church through faith development, I (Kay) have found that this is a very difficult process. The

---

7. Rick Warren, *The Purpose Driven Life* (Grand Rapids: Zondervan, 2002).

idea of creating a process rather than just choosing curriculum is such a new concept for the church. You are asking churches and their faith development teams to develop something that is nebulous. There is no one right way to do this. There are no concrete steps. I first try to help define a faith development process. I then provide them with samples of other churches' pathways (see the HCI website for samples). The team can quickly hit information overload. All of this results in not needing to spend more than an hour with the faith development team the first time they gather with me. At the first gathering with the team, the concept of a pathway is so new they don't even know what questions to ask! I oftentimes have to go back to the team a second time once they have had time to wrap their brains around the information, review some of the churches' pathways, and do some of the recommended reading. So give them some teaching time, but for the most part assign some reading to them. Many books have been listed in this section as resources. Pick two or three and have each team member read a different resource. In a couple of weeks, have the team come back together and share their findings with the one another. Only after they have had some time to digest some of the information will they begin to truly understand their task at hand.

Once the process is completed, the pastor and leaders are tasked with rolling out the process. It is helpful to include a personal evaluation that allows people to determine where they are in their spiritual journey. When the process is rolled out to the congregation, offer opportunities for people to engage in the process. It is best to roll out new opportunities to engage in intentional faith development at least twice a year, once in the spring and once in the fall. While it is optimal to have Sunday school classes engage in the faith development process when scheduling their teachings, it is not always possible. Some may be resistant to doing things differently. So engage people when and where you can, but just know not everyone will be on board. New people will come in under this process and that is most important.

After eight years in this process, it is still difficult to find churches that have done this well. Teams think it will be easy, but they find it difficult. Many times the pastor ends up finishing up the creation of the process. The team feels ill equipped or lacking the theological training to do such a thing. The churches usually don't make the prescription deadline. If they get the process in place, they don't roll it out well. They roll it out once, but it doesn't become a part of the life of the congregation.

Besides the resources cited in the prescriptions above, some other useful tools to review for developing your church's intentional faith development process are *Charting a Course of Discipleship*, *Move*, and *Growing True Disciples*.[8]

---

8. Teresa Gilbert, Patty Johansen, and Jay Regennitter, *Charting a Course Discipleship: A*

Case Studies

Case Study One

Another prescription was to increase discipleship training as a way to create openings for newcomers but to also deepen our member's understanding of being a disciple of Jesus Christ. We began last fall a program on Wednesday evening called "Wednesday Night Live." It features a fellowship supper from 5:00–6:00 p.m. that has been prepared beforehand; a thirty-minute worship service; and sixty- to ninety-minute long study groups. These groups range from Beth Moore Bible studies, to Financial Peace University, Stephen Ministry training, Core Methodist Beliefs, Marriage studies, Men's studies, and so on. Our fall session lasted ten weeks, and our winter session is eight weeks long. We take breaks in between sessions. We have probably averaged 125 people in attendance in our study groups. We attract people who worship only on Wednesday and not on Sunday for various reasons, which gives us another option to offer to people. —Mark Mildren, senior pastor of First UMC in West Plains, MO

Case Study Two

For adult intentional faith development, CUMC has made an interesting journey. Our HCI team developed an intentional faith development process known as The Quest, which provides for four different ways that adults (both college age and older) can connect to small groups, Sunday school, service projects, and so on. Those four ways are Explore, Connect, Grow, and Unleash. All of our existing small-group ministries were redefined as to which components of The Quest they belonged, and every new small group, whether through Christian education or service, is created with this intentional faith development classification in mind. We are now tracking participation numbers, finding that we have a good percentage of involvement in faith development with those who attend worship.

Probably the biggest achievement in our adult education process that was given impetus through HCI has been connecting adult Christian education and service under one umbrella, instead of having them as two separate (and competing) ministry areas. The hiring of a quarter-time director of discipleship ministries has been key. —Kevin Shelton, pastor of Community UMC in Columbia, MO

Workbook on Christian Discipleship (Nashville: Discipleship Resources, 2012); Greg Hawkins and Cally Parkinson, *Move: What 1,000 Churches Reveal about Spiritual Growth* (Grand Rapids: Zondervan, 2011); George Barna, *Growing True Disciples: New Strategies for Producing Genuine Followers of Christ* (Colorado Springs: WaterBrook, 2001).

Summary

	Compelling	Noncompelling
Leadership	Intentional, clear, written, and understood	Spotty, individual
Congregation	Known, visible, accessible	It's a mystery, informal, unclear
Community	There is a positive behavior change	Nonexistent, no difference between Christians and non-Christians

Group Questions

1. In your church, how does one get from being a guest to an authentic follower of Jesus Christ?

2. What does your leadership team believe are the marks of a disciple?

3. Describe your current discipleship pathway.

4. What percent of your congregation is involved in some sort of spiritual growth process? Is membership or discipleship your goal?

5. Share a time where you experienced a step forward in your faith development.

Connection Process

Prevailing Symptoms

Some of us have come to believe that if a person walks through the door, our "friendliness" will bring them back again and again. However, the historical decline in churches tells us this is not working well. The connection process is all about building relationships. The connection process starts with the introduction through hospitality and ends when a new believer/guest is connected in the life of the congregation and starting on his or her discipleship journey. In our HCI weekend consultations, we have continued to be surprised that many times the only connection made with a guest beyond worship is a formal form letter from the pastor sent out the following week.

If connecting to guests is a priority of the church, it is hard to imagine that sending a form letter from the pastor is the best authentic first step in building that relationship. If you are already a Christian and familiar with the mainline church, you may figure out on your own how to get connected beyond the Sunday morning experience. But, in most of our churches, the process of connecting is not very clear for both the church and the guest. It is a little like going to a new city and trying to operate their transit system. Our experience is that most large city transit systems are not particularly intuitive to a newcomer. You are left on your own to try to figure it out. Maybe you can get a few people to answer a few questions for you. Once you have figured it out, it sort of works for you. Most churches' connectional processes look like large city transit systems. They are just not very intuitive. We believe a good connection process is obvious, strategic, authentic, and simple. It needs to be designed with the end destination in mind. When we do find a connectional process in a church, it is tied into becoming a church member and then it stops. An assumption we make in HCI is that membership is not the final destination. It may be a step along the way, but it cannot be the end result. Discipleship needs to be the end result. The connectional process is the first step along the pathway of discipleship. The end result of a good connectional process is that guests become regular worship attenders, develop authentic relationships within the congregation, and become connected to a ministry.

A connectional process may begin at any point or time in the life of a congregation and in the life of an individual. In other words, a person could step into the life of the congregation through multiple entry points such as a life crisis, a class, a conversation at a coffee shop, an outwardly focused event, or a midweek children's event, to name a few. In fact, what we continue to learn is that first entry into the life of the church is often an alternate experience outside the Sunday morning experience. Compelling and competent congregations have developed a life pattern that makes it very easy for any person at any stage in life to find an entry point. In fact, those churches have become very sensitive to the needs of people outside their congregation. Becoming sensitive to the needs of people outside your congregation is the first step in the connection process. Having multiple entry points during the life and week of a congregation is the key to the beginning of a good connectional process. It doesn't do any good to make people sensitive to the needs of the community if there are not multiple entry points for people to experience something authentic and new.

But it is still true in most churches that the primary entry point for guests in the connectional process is the Sunday morning experience. Yet, most of these are geared toward the believer and are not necessarily geared toward helping a first-time guest enter the connectional process. The Sunday morning experiences are designed for fellowship, classroom teaching, and a worship service that fits our likes and preferences. Very few seasoned disciples show up thinking their task is about helping someone else take a step in their connectional journey. One example of not making ourselves available for guests' next step is congregants being in Sunday school right up until church begins—or even coming out late. Another example is being tied up in choir or band practice and not noticing a guest. We are so busy getting ready and preparing ourselves for worship, we don't notice the guests in our midst. There is no built-in time for connectional ministries to occur. We often see Sunday as about us rather than about being prepared for and having the expectation of receiving and connecting with guests. The second step of the connection process starts with extravagant hospitality, which involves every one of us who is a disciple (see chapter 2). Sunday morning is not just about me. It is about others.

Besides the customary pastoral follow-up form letter, we often lack "what's next." After the letter is sent, we don't have a plan for what happens if the guest returns for a second visit or a third visit. Or what is the next step if the guest does not return? Not only do we not have actions outlined, we also have no intentional process to implement.

As we said earlier, it is a common misunderstanding that any connection process leads people to membership. However, membership is not necessarily the desired outcome. It's great if it happens, but that is not the goal. The first goal is to connect with a guest relationally so that we are the bridge that allows the person to know Christ. As we are thinking through this process, we need to be careful that this is truly a connection process and not a process to "sell" the church and God. People don't need or want a sales pitch. Rather, a connection process assists guests and new believers to find a place in ministry and start on their discipleship journey. Our job is to help the person connect with the life of the congregation. This really turns most systems in place upside down. Many connectional systems that we have encountered offer people a church menu rather than a connection process and "connector" in hopes that they would find their place. We recommend using "connectors," which are persons or teams leading the connection process, who will ask questions of the guests to better know them and foster a better connection into the life of the congregation. In fact, a good connectional process journeys with people until they step into the discipleship pathway. It is the difference in a travel agent and a tour guide. The travel agent gives you the menu and suggests trips to take. The tour guide goes on the trip with you. We need our connectors to be tour guides, not travel agents.

Churches without a connection process also lack a group of people building authentic relationships. The connection process is most often seen as only the "pastor's job" and lacks a team of people who have the gift and heart to build relationships with the unchurched. There is usually a lack of accountability anywhere in the life of the congregation for a connection process to exist, let alone be implemented.

If guests come back for a second visit, there is definitely some interest on their behalf. Yet if we have no process for building relationships and helping them find their way to a relationship with Christ, they won't stick around. So if you have people who show some interest, but then fade away, you might just have a connection process failure on your hands. Many times the seed for a possible connection is planted prior to the worship experience. However, if that seed is not fertilized after worship while they are still in the building or with a follow-up within twenty-four hours, the connection seed will likely not be fertilized and grow. We have to nurture that fragile new relationship. Remember, it isn't about selling our church; it's about offering an authentic relationship and grace.

Our mystery worshipper reports often reflect a lack of connection processes. Guests are left to fend for themselves after worship. Congregants are finished with worship and connecting with other friends in the congregation making lunch plans. The guests are left with the lack of opportunity to connect in a different or deeper way.

While some churches have a connection process for guests for worship experiences, most churches oftentimes struggle with a connection process to connect with people for any other time of the week. Churches have opportunities that offer the chance for relationship building including bridge events, elbow activities (social activities connecting the churched with unchurched people), as well as the pastors' and congregants' personal contacts throughout the week in the life of the church (see chapter 3). And yet most opportunities go untapped and unrecognized. Outside of Sunday morning, we seldom think of the connection process as an opportunity to connect people to relationships and then their faith journey.

We run into many people who wish and want their church to be friendlier and more connected. Yet they are unsure what they can personally do to make this happen. This is especially true when many of our congregants are not necessarily extroverts. We have discovered there is one thing that every person can do. They can pray up the names of new people. Often our churches have a prayer team that is very inwardly focused on the joys and concerns of the congregants. Those churches struggling with connection don't have a prayer team focused on the unchurched, guests, and community. They have not imagined praying for people that are new. They have also not imagined expanding their team to include more people. A healthy connectional process includes a prayer team for the names of new people and those whose names we don't know yet. We don't want to underestimate the power of connectors, praying for new people, and leaders trying to make this happen (see the introduction about prayer).

Prescriptions

Example One

A connection team of three to four people will be assembled by the pastor, in consultation with the coach, on or before [date]. With the assistance of the coach, the connection team will create a process to help new people connect into the life of the congregation.

The connection process includes the following:

⊕ Connecting with people at bridge events (building relationships)

⊕ Connecting guests when they attend worship (relationships and ministries)

✚ Connecting seasoned believers of Jesus Christ (intentional faith development)

The process encourages a guest to find a connection in a ministry or small group to begin their discipleship journey. The process will be created and put into place no later than [date].

Example Two

The administrative board in conjunction with the staff/pastor-parish relations committee will find a highly capable paid or unpaid staff member to serve as a director of hospitality and connections. The new director, in conjunction with the administrative board chair and the pastor, will recruit, equip, and empower a team to lead the congregation in achieving radical hospitality and connecting people into the life of the church. The goal will be to have this person and their team in place by [date]. The following books will be used as key resources: *Beyond the First Visit* and *Fusion.*[1]

The pastor and the coach will put together a job description that will include the following:

✚ Making sure inside and outside signage provide clear directions and times for all those visiting the church for the first time

✚ Reviewing and recommending that communications, website, and social media provide a clear and consistent message both internally and externally

✚ Recruiting and training volunteers

✚ Developing a new process for connecting guests to the life of the church

✚ Making recommendations to the administrative board that ensures facilities are consistent with hospitality goals

✚ Following up on all first-time guests and on those who have been attending but have missed a certain number of weeks

---

1. Gary L. McIntosh, *Beyond the First Visit: The Complete Guide to Connecting Guests to Your Church* (Grand Rapids: Baker Books, 2006); Nelson Searcy, *Fusion: Turning First Time Guests into Fully-Engaged Members of Your Church* (Ventura, CA: Regal, 2007).

Remedy

The first step after assembling a connection team is for the coach to train the team. The team will be taught about best practices of churches with an intentional connectional process. A great first step is for the team to study together the book *Beyond the First Visit* by Gary McIntosh to truly start understanding the connection process.

The next step is for the team to begin to create a process of what happens after a person is a guest in worship the first time, second time, third time, and so on. They must also decide the next steps for guests encountered at bridge events and in the community in general. Each step must be assigned to a particular person or position. Each person must be held accountable. Those serving on the connection team may be great at creating the process, but you may find the spiritual gifts in doing the work to be among other people. Make sure your connection process also includes steps for those not returning for a second visit.

I (Kay) find it very helpful for the pastor to identify a few people with the gifts of relationship building. We refer to this person as a connector. These people are ones that others feel extremely comfortable around. They have a natural instinct of reading the guest's body language and knowing what questions are suitable for the time and step in the relationship. They know how much is enough and how much is too much. When a greeter spots a guest, the greeter hands the guest off to a connector. The connector is then the ambassador for that guest for the day and for later visits. The connector serves the guest a cup of coffee, shows him or her around the facility, sits with the guest in worship, introduces the guest to others who share commonalities with the guest, offers to take him or her to lunch, introduces him or her to the pastor, follows up with a phone call, seeks the same guest out the next Sunday, and helps him or her find a place to connect in the life of the congregation. The connector builds a relationship with the guest over time—getting to know him or her and how best to connect him or her to a small group. Remember, this isn't about selling the church's programs or ministries. The connector is charged with helping the guest first connect with other people, then to a small group, and thus into a relationship with Christ. Too often we think of getting the guest to become a member rather than offering first a relationship with ourselves that is the bridge to a relationship with Christ.

> So we are ambassadors who represent Christ. God is negotiating with you through us. We beg you as Christ's representatives, "Be reconciled to God!" (2 Cor 5:20)

I (Bob) had an interesting discovery in the Wesley Heritage Tour in England. While at the "New Room" in Bristol, I learned that John Wesley would ask his class leaders and other more mature disciples to strategically place themselves among the congregation for worship. He instructed them to follow up with anybody they noticed who seemed to be engaged in the message and invite them to that week's class meeting (small group gathering) to go deeper and take next steps. Isn't it interesting that Wesley (two hundred years ago) had thought through a connectional process? Wesley understood that the laity's role was much more than just coming and being spiritually fed. In fact, their role was to be active participants in helping others go deeper into their faith.

The connection process is a team approach that is laity driven. If guests only connect to the pastor, the church will never have sustained growth past one hundred or so people in attendance. Guests need to be able to connect with others in the congregation who have shared interests and experiences. Congregants connecting with guests create a kingdom multiplication opportunity. Guests connecting only with the pastor create a family system that is pastor centered with limited growth potential. The more missional church model of today would lend itself to a much broader laity involvement and moves away from the pastor-centered spoke-and-wheel operation of the mainline church.

Case Study

Connection Plan Draft from Blue Ridge Boulevard UMC in Kansas City, MO

First Visit

When guests arrive at [church name], they will be met with radical hospitality. We will be genuine and friendly, doing the unexpected to make guests feel welcome and valued. The greeters will welcome them in and introduce them to connectors. The connectors will then offer them refreshments, introduce them to the pastor (if available), offer a tour of the building (sanctuary, coat room, bathroom, classroom, and so on), offer to sit with them in worship, and answer any questions (as appropriate and contextual for each unique visitor). The connectors' responsibility is to build relationships with the guests and engage in meaningful conversations to gain an understanding of the needs, gifts, and desires of the guests and how best to connect them to a small group or ministry in the church.

A list of connectors will be at the welcome center with at least one connector on duty each Sunday. The usher coordinator will use the blue cards or other methods to also identify guests during or after the church service.

First Visit

That afternoon, the connector assigned to that guest will go to the guest's home and present him or her with a welcome packet gift (at the door/don't go in/thank them for coming/connector contact info). Within forty-eight hours, the connector will send a handwritten note expressing gratitude for the guest's attendance and indicating that the connector will be anxiously watching for him or her the following Sunday. The connector actively prays for the guest. That connector will continue to be assigned to that guest until he or she is through the guest process as defined in this plan.

Pastor Contact

After the first visit, depending on the information the guest provides, the pastor will contact the guest via phone, e-mail, or by handwritten note to welcome and acknowledge his or her presence.

Second Visit

The connector will be watching/attentive to the possibility of the guest's arrival. The connector will again offer to give a tour of the building, introduce the guest to others (including the pastor if the guest did not meet him or her the previous week), and ask if he or she has questions.

Third Visit

The connector will be watching/attentive to the possibility of the guest's arrival. The connector will offer to take the guest for lunch or coffee after church and conduct an informal interview to gather information from the guest, making sure to ask, "What are your needs? How can we help?" Given the information from the informal conversation, the connector will be able to offer connection points within the church that meet the needs of the guest. If the guest seems interested in a particular group, the connector will contact the leader of that group with the guest's contact information for the leader to invite the guest to the next meeting/event. Some possible groups for the guest to join include the following:

- Sunday school

- United Methodist Women

- Prayer shawl ministry

- Choir

- Bells

- Wednesday Night Live

- Book club

- Boy/Girl Scouts

- Women's Bible study and issues group

- Card ministry

- Youth group

The Connection

The connector continues to check in with the guest and leader of the group that the guest is "trying out" until he or she becomes involved with a small group of some sort. Using the information gained in the informal interview and body language of the guest, the connector will suggest places to plug in or ask about creating new opportunities.

Connector Duties

- Be available at the main entrance for greeters to connect guests with you.

- Provide an authentic smile, greeting, and handshake (look them in the eye).

- Introduce yourself.

- Offer food/coffee.

- Have a sincere desire to build relationships with guests so that they might come to know Christ and become a part of the congregation to grow in their faith

- Read guests' body language to interpret their comfort level for interaction with the connector.

- Escort guests to locations they might be looking for (bathroom, children's wing, downstairs, and so on).

○ Be at the inside entrance by 9:30 am (9:45 am at the latest) until 10:05 am.

○ Wear the "Connector" blue ribbon. They are stored at the welcome desk.

○ Help the guest/member make a connection to activities going on at church beyond Sunday morning worship.

○ Greeters need to know how to read the guest to see what they are ready for.

○ Connect guests/members to a small group that meets their needs.

○ Stay with guests until they are actually plugged into a small group that meets regularly—then hand them off and follow up.

○ If the first group does not work, then assist the guests in finding another group.

○ Read *Beyond the First Visit* by Gary McIntosh and discuss it with the hospitality team to gain a full understanding of this role.

Bridge Events

The hospitality/connection team will work with the bridge events team to follow up with people who attended the bridge events (including handwritten notes, e-mails, or phone calls).

Summary

	Compelling	Noncompelling
Leadership	Intentionality	Pastor's job to connect
Congregation	There is a place for everyone, identify connectors	Sunday school classes are all we need
Community	Open doors to all in a variety of ways	Unconnected

Group Questions

1. What is the process in your church to help guests connect within the life of the congregation?

2. How does it feel to desire a connection to a person or group when that desire to connect is not shared by the other?

3. If the church holds a community event and collects names, what are the next steps after the event to build a relationship with those guests?

4. Identify people within your congregation who have the spiritual gifts of being highly relational.

5. Share a time in which you were new in a situation and you felt you were quickly connected to a group.

Leadership Development

Prevailing Symptoms

Developing leaders may be the one secret ingredient for compelling, competent congregations. Yet, it is one of the most overlooked secret ingredients. Until recently, there has not been an emphasis on leadership, and only very recently have we considered lay leadership development. In our lifetimes, there have always been some tools available to help laity identify spiritual gifts, assess their time and talents, and identify their strengths. But, at the end of the day, assessment tools were used as a means to fill the slots of the committee vacancies in a given calendar year. Truth be told, for most pastors, including myself (Bob), the process of leadership development looked like this:

I showed up in the fall with a nominations committee. I distributed a pictorial directory to every committee member. I distributed the sheet with the vacancies for the church committees. We started looking through the pictorial and our memories to find people to fill in the blanks. The names were then divided up amongst the team to call over the next week to ask the person to serve. The committee person making the call would assure the person asked to fill the vacancy that it wouldn't take much time or effort. The nominations team then gathered the following week to see which vacancies we still had in the committee slots. The team would then resort to filling the vacancies with people we know and who we know will always serve. If we did any training at all, we would send them to a "My Job" district workshop (the denominational workshop on learning the duties of the job in which they were elected to serve) to learn about their particular committee. Then they were sent back to the church to do their job. Most likely this was the extent of their leadership development.

As a result, the system gets what the system is designed to get. Then we wonder why this isn't working very well. We wonder why are leaders are not equipped. In the past ten years, stacks of leadership books have been written that focus on church leadership, but our experience is that these books still haven't changed the way we identify and equip leaders at the local church level. Maybe we have read the books, but we haven't applied it. We have seen a new emphasis on clergy and laity in peer learning communities. But we still struggle at church to build effective lay leadership.

The number one stumbling block in creating a lay leadership development plan is time. We often find a pastor buried in the day-to-day operations, covered up with a never-ending to-do list, and suffering from the burden of carrying an inwardly focused church. That pastor can hardly imagine where he or she could come up with three to five hours per month to invest in a group of people who may or may not be leaders or be the right leaders to fill the committee vacancies. Furthermore, it is hard for laity to imagine spending three to five hours a month in a lay leadership classes, reading books to become leaders in an organization that isn't going anywhere. Often competent leaders don't feel it is worth their time, effort, and talents to invest in a system that looks fairly broken. They feel it is a waste of time. We have to start hiring people to do ministry for us when we can't break the cycle of poor leadership development. In fact, we didn't even realize we were in this cycle. One of the outcries we hear in consultations is that the church doesn't have enough volunteers. This is the result of this broken leadership development system. If ministry ideas are dreamed and created but there is a broken leadership development system, these same ideas and dreams will go up in smoke and lead to further frustration and convince competent lay leaders not to get involved. The only way to break this cycle is to create a true leadership development plan.

Leadership development does not occur by osmosis. Leadership development does not happen by sitting on a committee. Leaders are identified, equipped, and nurtured through an intentional leadership development process. When there is no true leadership development plan, there is usually a lack of understanding of the job and commitment when a person agrees to a volunteer position. There is certainly little evaluation of their qualification for the job. Many times people say yes graciously and then we float on luck. We are using a guessing system rather than an intentional leadership development process. When there is not a true development system, it leads to lots of guesswork. The nominations committee is guessing whether somebody has the strength, gifts, or spiritual temperament to do a certain job. Often, when you are on the nominations committee, you are relying on personal relationships to fill the vacancies. And even then, you are still guessing if those people are good matches for those positions in the life of the church.

> ## You only grow a church by as much as you grow your leadership.

Congregations that fail in leadership development are also limiting the size of the congregation. It is a stranglehold on the life of the congregation. A lack of leadership development knocks out the competent leaders from engaging in the church and does not give them the opportunity to use their gifts for the church. Remember the book *Good to Great* by Jim Collins?[1] There is a chapter devoted to getting the right people on the bus, the right combination of people on the team. That is very true. In a volunteer organization like the church, getting the right people in the right seats, the right job for each person on the team, is even more important. Without a leadership development process, you will never get the right people on the bus—let alone get them in the right seats. Even with a leadership development process, it is difficult. Without a system, it is impossible. People are oftentimes placed on committees based on tradition, common personalities, popularity, and availability rather than by matching people's gifts and skills with the needed gifts and skills of the positions. When the board/council does not devote any time to leadership development as part of their regular meeting agenda, they become a part of the bottleneck of the church's ability to grow. Instead, the board/council may end up focusing on managing the day-to-day operations of the church and not devoting time to seeing the big picture.

Prescriptions

Example One

An intentional process will be put in place to identify, raise up, and equip existing and future leaders for the church. Not only will leadership development become a priority for all paid and unpaid staff, the committee on nominations and lay leadership will develop a plan to identify, recruit, and train potential leaders for the church's ministries. This plan will be developed and implemented on or before [date].

---

1. Jim Collins, *Good to Great: Why Some Companies Make the Leap . . . and Others Don't* (New York: HarperCollins, 2001).

Example Two

The pastor, with assistance from the coach, will develop an intentional leadership development pathway to identify, equip, and place leaders in leadership roles. This will be an ongoing process to add leadership depth to the congregation. Leadership classes will commence on or before [date] and be led by [name of pastor].

Not only will leadership development become a priority for all paid and unpaid staff, the nominations and lay leadership committee will develop a plan to identify, recruit, and train potential leaders for the church's ministries. This plan will be in place no later than [date].

Remedy

Many times, the first step in leadership development is to continuously offer both pastors and laity the opportunity to learn together in community with one another. In larger churches, the pastors gather with other pastors to learn while laity gather at another place and time with other laity. In smaller churches, the learning is done with the pastor and laity of one church in the same room with pastors and laity from other small churches. The biggest takeaway from this experience is the feeling and understanding that one church is not experiencing these things in isolation. Other churches have similar experiences and struggles. They offer support, best practices, and friendships with one another. There is often a resulting feeling of hopefulness. Whether the gathering is the larger churches or the smaller, the imperative step is for the participants of the learning groups to come back to church and share what they learned, their takeaways, and the next steps. For if all we do is learn and never implement, why did we invest our time and energy to attend these learning groups? The participants are encouraged to create action steps and implementation between the larger group gatherings. In the Missouri Conference of The UMC, we initially called these continuous learning communities *pastoral leadership development* (PLD) and *lay leadership development* (LLD) (see the HCI website for materials for these learning communities).

For churches that develop leaders, every board/council meeting has leadership development as part of their agenda each and every time they meet. These churches value leadership development and take every opportunity to develop current leaders as well as invest in the leaders of the next generation. Pastors and those responsible for placing people in leadership positions (i.e., nominations or lay leadership committees) identify the next group or generation of leaders and pour into them before they are asked to step into leadership. Thus leaders step into their roles fully equipped for the job at hand rather than having to receive on-the-job training (or most likely no training at all). In addition to having new leaders ready for vacant leadership positions, the church is more likely to better match the leader with the position if the pastor has spent time with the potential leader getting to know his or her personality, gifts, talents, interests, and experiences.

It is extremely important for the leadership team to participate in an annual retreat. The annual retreat creates the opportunity for concentrated leadership development and focused time to work, expand, and live into the church's mission and vision work. It also provides a great opportunity for the seasoned leaders to mentor and pour themselves into the new and next generation leaders. This is also an opportune time to do annual planning.

Churches that develop good leaders create opportunities for growth. This includes investing in leadership development by budgeting for leadership development. These opportunities must be for both the pastor and laity including existing leaders and the next generation of leaders. Leadership development can occur by going to leadership events, visiting healthy and growing churches, bringing in speakers and consultants, and investing in a coach for your pastor and leaders.

In addition to unpaid leaders of the church, there are many churches that have no intentional plans, means, or expectations of developing their paid leaders. How are we investing in today's leaders so they will still be equipped to lead the church of the future? Not only are we oftentimes missing an intentional process to raise our paid leaders (staff), we are often missing an employee evaluation process. Paid staff members are missing job descriptions, goals, and objectives. And, at all levels, we have no accountability and lack the importance, implementation, and understanding of accountability.

Leadership development must include adopting accountable leadership. Accountable leadership combines responsibility and authority to hold one another accountable. Clear lines of reporting must first be in place before accountability can begin. We must also learn that accountable leadership is not to be used as a weapon but rather as a mentoring, encouraging relationship to bring out the best in people while still holding them accountable for their job descriptions as well as the church goals and objectives. When implemented properly, the accountable leadership model is very healthy, empowering, and effective. For more information on accountable leadership, we recommend the book *Winning on Purpose* by John Edmund Kaiser.[2]

Here is one method that I (Bob) used that might transition your current nominations or lay leadership committee leadership system into a more intentional leadership development plan:

---

2. John Edmund Kaiser, *Winning on Purpose: How to Convince Congregations to Succeed in their Mission* (Nashville: Abingdon Press, 2006).

⊕ Gather the nominations or lay leadership committee in the fall to compile a list of twenty-five to thirty names of people not currently in leadership.

⊕ Invite those people by letter and phone call to an orientation meeting in September.

⊕ Outline an eight-month curriculum (syllabus) along with the requirements for participation and present it at the orientation. The class would be three hours once a month.

⊕ Ask each potential leader at orientation to notify the pastor if he or she is interested in pursuing the class. About fifteen of the twenty-five will probably say yes. The group should pick a time each week to gather at someone's home to share a meal. The hosting responsibility should rotate through the group. The participants will discuss a book each time.

⊕ For the first class, buy the books for the leaders. Thereafter, the leaders should buy their own books. You will use approximately six books over the course of the eight months. The agenda is simple: share devotion and prayer as well as joys and concern, and discuss the books. The pastor should ask three questions about each book: What in this book really got your attention? What in this book really drove you crazy (that you didn't like)? Was there anything in this book that applies to our church at this time? All participants should write their answers on a whiteboard. I (Bob) quickly learned that they did not read the books, so I handed out my version of Cliff's Notes about the three questions as I saw them and summarized the key points of the book. The group made no decisions. They took no action. This was simply a class. The meeting ended with prayer, often utilizing different prayer techniques.

⊕ Each participant completed the StrengthsFinder, DISC, and spiritual gifts assessments.

⊕ Conclude the group in the spring with individual interviews with the pastor. The group experience, assessments, and interviews are then used by the pastor and nominations committee in selecting the new group of leaders for the upcoming year. It is possible that only half of your participants will become leaders. Some may realize that they

aren't equipped to lead; others may leave the church because they don't like where the church is headed. It is important to mix existing leaders into the class to infuse new blood and new ideas into the present leadership regime. You have to be careful not to overwhelm the group with existing leaders, but at the same time you are trying to make inroads into the existing system to think in a new direction. A mistake you can make here is to have all existing leaders go through leadership development. Bring those select few existing leaders along with the new people.

I (Bob) readily admit I was in a situation with an influx of new people in a growing church. I also admit that in the first couple of years at Church of the Shepherd, I didn't have new people. I had to first work on the more pressing issues (see the previous chapters) before I could really work intently on leadership development. I had to get to the foundational things (mission, vision, worship, and hospitality) working well and getting new people in first before I could go about developing new leaders. Note: Leadership development is not step one in an existing church! It is critical but not the first prescription to implement.

Case Study

Barnabas was a leader in the early church who mentored the apostle Paul after Paul's conversion. They shared in ministry for several seasons before going their separate ways. Barnabas means "son of encouragement." Barnabas mentored other leaders including John Mark. He offers as biblical connection with our desire to develop leaders in the church today.

At Christ UMC, Kay Kotan and I created a Barnabas Group. We invited a number of young adults in the church to explore their faith with others; to grow their understanding of themselves to God and the church; and to identify their gifts for ministry and leadership in order to more faithfully serve Jesus Christ. The goal was personal growth, which would benefit their personal and professional lives as well as cultivate them as leaders in the church.

Our experience was limited but positive. For the eight or ten people who participated in the nine-month group experience, it was an enriching experience. We spent time on scripture, prayer, personality and spiritual gift inventories, and discussion of leadership and the mission of the church. One couple in the group became dissatisfied with the slowness of change in our congregation and found another church. Others in the group continued their involvement in various congregational ministries.

Our decision to enter the Healthy Church Initiative precluded a follow-up group. We had a hundred people involved with intense study and discussion about

our congregational identity and need for change. All of our energy went into that process.

Looking back, my learnings about intentional leadership development included the following: To effectively cultivate leaders in a local church, the congregation needs a clear mission, vision, and core values. The clarity of mission is needed to provide guidance and support for developing leaders. Current leaders in the church need to be invested in walking with people through various levels of participation with increasing responsibility and authority for leadership. Without that shared vision of encouragement and willingness to invest energy in helping new leaders emerge, intentional ministries like a Barnabas Group will be frustrated.

At Central UMC, I have several leaders who understand the need to encourage others by walking with them in the development of ministries. One couple in particular invites people to their home for meals with the pastor to develop relationships. These personal connections foster trust and openness to invitations to share in the responsibility for a new ministry. In incubating ministries, they invest their time and energy for conversation with new leaders about what is needed for faithful, effective ministry. They articulate and model the core values of the church's mission. Intentional leadership development begins with pastoral conversations with leaders who "get it" and informally devote themselves to such modeling and encouragement.

I believe such efforts are a prelude that will create an environment where a fresh approach to a Barnabas Group–type ministry might thrive. As we move in this direction at Central UMC, I want to include a component of peer mentoring. I will ask six established mentors of the church along with six newer persons...all of whom will benefit from this kind of group. We will ask established members to covenant with new members and meet with each other between each formal session to discuss the content of the group and encourage each other in the faith journey. Like the mentoring with confirmation classes, these relationships will continue long after the formal Barnabas process has concluded.

The Barnabas Group will meet seven times in the course of a year. Each session will have a particular focus/agenda for personal and spiritual development. Group members will be asked to bear the expense of several books and resources during the course of the year. The sessions will include an introduction to the faith journey and spiritual life; scripture, prayer, and service; a session about their own core beliefs or credo; a session about personality type and its significance for leading groups; two experiential sessions on leadership; and a final half day summary retreat.

For a Barnabas Group ministry to be fruitful, it must be sustained over several years. Succeeding groups of established members sharing with new members will provide a level of awareness and commitment to the church's mission and core values that will begin to permeate and energize the congregation. —Dr. Jim Simpson, lead pastor of Central UMC in Kansas City, MO

Summary

	Compelling	Noncompelling
Leadership	Commitment, on-board	Shortage of volunteers
Congregation	Role models	Not an open door for new people
Community	Upstanding, caring pillars of the community	The church has leaders?

Group Questions

1. How does one go about becoming a leader in your congregation?

2. What are the responsibilities of leadership in your congregation?

3. What is the process used by your nominations committee to fill committee positions each year?

4. What is your budget for leadership development?

5. Who is a leader you admire and why?

Strategic Ministry Planning

Prevailing Symptoms

How are decisions made at your church? In most of our HCI consultations, we have discovered that most decision making is haphazard at best. Most of a church's committee time is consumed in receiving reports of what has already been accomplished. A great deal of the committee time is spent in fellowship and storytelling while very little time is spent on helping their part of the church accomplish the mission and vision. In fact, in most churches we have consulted, very few people on the committees had much of an idea of what the mission and vision were let alone engaged in a decision-making process that aligned to that mission and vision. Rather, there is usually a very informal decision-making process in place. Committees typically manage how things have already been done. When decisions for our churches are not based on living into the vision to accomplish the mission of making disciples or any stated goals or objectives for the year, it is very hard to know if the church is actually accomplishing anything beyond merely existing.

When our churches lack strategic ministry planning, it is difficult to have alignment and know if they have accomplished their goals when there are no stated or known goals. In the absence of strategic planning, the unstated plan becomes simply existing and trying to get from one year to the next without any further decline in resources, time, and energy. The lack of strategic planning becomes more obvious when there begins to be a decline in people, energy, and resources. Often our solution is to try harder doing the things we have always done. Then frustration sets in and we often reach for some magic program. We grasp at straws believing that if we just did this, had this, built that, hired the right person, or had the right pastor, then we would suddenly have new energy and vitality in the church. It has been our experience that sometimes the HCI process has been treated as just another program to try. Then, if that doesn't work, there is something to blame. All of these are symptoms of a congregation that lacks strategic ministry planning.

During our HCI consultations, we often look for signs of whether the mission and vision are known throughout the congregation. One of the signs that the leadership is trying to embed the mission and vision is seeing it printed in multiple places like agendas, the website, bulletins, and newsletters. We are also looking for whether the leaders can verbally articulate the mission and vision and how their decision-making process ties into that mission and vision. We often see a church with good intentions work through the mission and vision statement, but yet the ministries lack alignment to those stated words. In addition, the implementation of the stated mission and vision in the various ministries is very difficult for congregations. Churches seldom evaluate the stated goals and whether they have really aligned the ministries to the mission and vision. Most of the time churches are evaluating ministries on whether they like them or don't like them, whether they align with their own personal interests and preferences, or who is running the ministry. Rarely do churches evaluate on if they are accomplishing the goals or if those goals are in alignment with the mission and vision.

Through our HCI consultation process, our experience has been that churches do not strategically plan their ministries. Rather, they are driven by calendar and tradition. Events are planned by copying last year's calendar onto this year's calendar. If any decisions are based on doing something, they are rarely based on goals, mission, and vision. Rather, they are based on the tradition of "that's what we have always done." The effectiveness of the ministry rarely enters into the decision-making process unless the church is struggling to get help to pull off said ministry.

Many churches have no identifiable goals or strategies. Therefore they spend most of their time concentrating on the day-to-day operations of the church. When a church lacks strategic planning, the leaders revert to fiduciary responsibilities (i.e., management). For example, when the trustee committee meets in a church without strategic ministry planning (where the mission and vision are not widely known) the committee will take up fiduciary responsibilities. It is easier to take on the technical conversations and changes rather than adaptive conversations and changes. It is easier to talk about fixing the sidewalk rather than how the building lends itself toward making disciples. By the time the committee figures out the sidewalk problem, they have exhausted their available time working on technical change and conversation. Another way to state this is that if we as a congregation don't have a target, it is hard to hit it.

Without a strategic plan, it is hard to get everyone moving in the same direction. You can have a stated mission and vision hanging on the wall, but without clear, obvious, and measurable steps for individuals, staff, committees, and teams, it is hard to imagine anyone moving forward. It looks like they should be able to, but when there is no identifiable target, everyone is moving in a variety of directions with good intentions and feeling as if they are accomplishing something. Without a set of goals, we revert to a 1980s mentality where we perceive a busy 24/7 program church as being an effective church. This has led to a mentality of us trying to be everything to everybody. We do lots of ministries, programs, and activities, but we don't do anything extremely well. We often ask in our consultations what their church does best. This is often a difficult question for people to answer. One of the outcomes of a church with no strategic plan is no one signature ministry is known to the community. I (Bob) often say this leads to a church being an inch deep and a mile wide.

When a church has no strategic ministry plan, the staff is most often driven by the urgent need of the moment to fill a ministry gap rather than be driven by the bigger picture—the mission and vision. Staffing decisions are based on ministry gaps or a ministry that no one else is willing to do. Many times, staff function is driven by the desires of the congregation rather than by the desire to accomplish the stated mission and vision of the church. Staff (both paid and unpaid) are not given goals and objectives based on the mission and vision to direct their day-to-day functions, objectives, and priorities. We rarely find churches that evaluate, train, or help staff understand their goals and objectives. Often, staff are hired because we like them, they have a personal need that the job might help, or they are part of the local family church system. When this hiring practice occurs, it makes it very difficult to evaluate and terminate ineffective staff. It is absolutely critical that we have a strategic plan so that we can hire personnel that assist and equip the church in accomplishing the strategic plan. Therefore, it allows the church to evaluate the personnel on how well they are accomplishing the strategic plan. The biggest obstacle to becoming a compelling and competent church is the inability of staff (paid and unpaid) to fully implement a strategic plan. The biggest reason that the HCI process succeeds or not centers on the ability of the pastor, laity, and staff to implement a plan. When implementation doesn't exist or goes badly, everything comes apart.

The ability to align and implement is key.

Prescriptions

Example One

Upon acceptance of this report (should that be the case), [church name] will adopt the mission "to make new disciples of Jesus Christ for the transformation of the world." On or before [date], the coach will conduct a day of visioning with the congregation. The vision statement will be cast by the pastor and blessed by leadership on or before [date]. The coach will conduct a strategic planning retreat with the pastor and new church board/council on or before [date]. The purpose of this retreat will be to train the leaders and create annual church ministry goals that are aligned with the new vision and mission.

Example Two

The coach will conduct a retreat for the pastor, new simplified board, and all paid staff on or before [date]. This retreat will include training for the new board on the simplified structure model, in which the four administrative committees (finance, trustees, staff/pastor-parish relations, and church council) combine into one team of ten to fifteen people; accountability leadership model; and strategic ministry planning. Planning for [year] will also take place at this retreat.

The pastor, in consultation with the coach and new board, will evaluate current paid staff in order to align staff with the mission, vision, goals, and financial resources of the church on or before [date].

Example Three

The pastor, in consultation with the coach, will implement an annual planning process that will set three church-wide goals, as well as goals for individual ministries and goals for any paid and unpaid staff. The coach will work with the pastor, the ministry team leaders, and the administrative board to establish an evaluation process to use with the ministry teams to make sure they are fulfilling the mission and the vision of the church. This will be accomplished by the [fall or spring] of [year]. The administrative board will receive quarterly updates as to the progress of the ministry goals and will take the responsibility for the implementation of the three church-wide goals.

Example Four

The pastor, in conjunction with the coach, will appoint a mission audit team. The audit team shall conduct a mission audit of all the ministries of the church. Ministries not fulfilling the mission of the church will be given a calendar year to be redesigned in order to implement the mission or be discontinued. This mission audit must be completed by [date].

Remedy

The first step in the strategic ministry planning process is to adopt the mission (for more on this, see chapter 1). In our work, we believe the mission has been given to us in Matthew 28:19-20, the Great Commission, and is "to make disciples of Jesus Christ for the transformation of the world." This is the reason churches exist. This is the purpose of the church. Everything a church does must be based on this purpose of its existence. In the Missouri Conference of The United Methodist Church, the first thing the HCI consultation team does is to ask the congregation to adopt the mission statement of The United Methodist Church. The mission statement is constant. The mission never changes. We do not need to revisit the mission statement. We are simply commissioned to do it!

The second step in the strategic ministry planning process is to cast the vision (for more on casting the vision, also see chapter 1). This is a workshop experience that includes teaching time, a prayer walk, reflection time, and small group work on rough drafts of the vision statement. The pastor then takes what he or she heard, experienced, and saw in the workshop for prayer and discernment. The pastor then casts a final version of the vision statement for a blessing from the leaders. This entire process should take no longer than one or two months.

Once the mission is adopted and the visioning process is followed and confirmed by the leadership team, the leaders are ready for their strategic ministry planning. This is a sequential process. Your church must adopt the mission and finish the visioning process before strategic planning can begin. There are many ways to do strategic planning. In our experience, one of the best ways to do this is to have an annual planning retreat. Depending on the size of the church, the planning retreat can take on many forms (e.g., staff only, laity only, staff and laity together). The size of your church really matters here. The smaller the church, the more participation you need from everyone. The larger the church, the more participation will be role-based.

A word of caution: when you are proceeding in developing your strategic plan, you need to understand church by size dynamics and how to proceed. If you lack this understanding, please get the appropriate counsel (e.g., HCI website) before proceeding. If you choose the wrong method of strategic planning, the process could backfire. In our experience, a great time to complete this strategic planning is the early fall if your church operates on the January to December calendar. If your church's cycle is more of an August through July timeframe, you want your annual strategic ministry planning retreat in the spring. This is also a great time to bring together existing leaders and new leaders for the upcoming year or season. I (Kay) prefer to take the leaders offsite and optimally out of town for this experience. Most times it is an overnight experience in a retreat setting so that leaders can unplug from everyday life and fully immerse themselves in the experience. Meal preparation is completed by small groups within the leadership team to promote collaboration and cooperation. Spiritual formation, communion, prayer, team building exercises, and reflection time are all key elements in this experience in addition to the learning and planning.

At the first strategic ministry planning leadership retreat, the core values must be identified. The core values speak to the DNA of your church. They are guiding principles. They are present even if they have never been identified. These are the things that your church holds near and dear. These values are what guide decisions in your church whether they are stated or not. It is important to clearly identify and articulate these values. They provide the boundaries for clear decision making while living out the vision and mission. Examples of core values are preaching and teaching scripture, prayer, tradition, community, fellowship, encouragement, excellence, family, giving, leadership, and innovation. Most times, when church leadership goes through the process of identifying their core values, they also identify a value they aspire to become. This is especially true of declining or stagnant congregations that begin to realize some of their core values may indeed be leading to their decline. About five values are usually sufficient in describing the church. (See the HCI website for the Core Values Audit worksheet and directions.)

At this point in the strategic ministry planning process, the leaders should fully understand the mission, vision, and core values. This would be an excellent time to introduce how all five pieces of the strategic ministry planning fit together. The five pieces of a complete strategic ministry plan are mission, vision, core values, goals, and strategies. This is also a great time to take a step back to look at how all five pieces of strategic planning interrelate and gain a clear insight on who is responsible for what so that you can assign accountability for outcomes, which is essential if you are to evaluate your personnel, ministry, and pastor in the coming year. The model of accountability will be talked about in chapter 9.

Here is a possible organizational structure diagram. The first diagram shows the five elements of strategic ministry planning. The second diagram shows an organizational chart. The third diagram illustrates how the first two diagrams (systems) interrelate to one another.

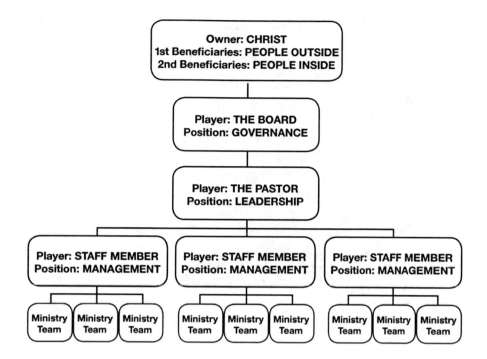

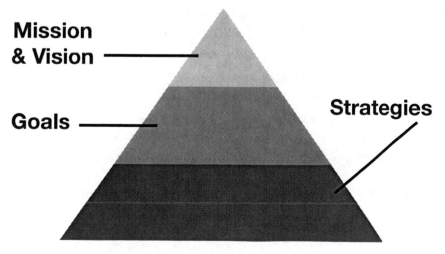

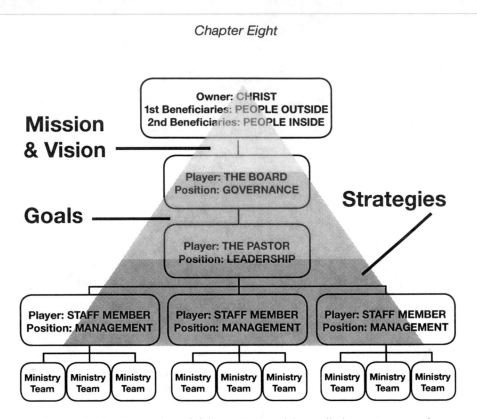

When leadership and staff fully understand how all these pieces work together, everyone begins to see how their piece of ministry ties into the bigger pictures. Often when I (Kay) conduct strategic ministry planning, this is where "aha" moments occur. People get it! Everyone is working for a common purpose. Everyone is rowing in the same direction. This becomes the sweet spot where effective ministry can happen in compelling and competent congregations.

Once the mission, vision, core values, and overview are complete, it is time to start working on goals. Goals are the three to five "big picture" activities the church would like to accomplish in the upcoming year to live more fully into the vision and accomplish the mission. Goals are the stepping-stones into our preferred future (our vision). We want to make sure that these three church-wide goals obviously support the mission and vision of the church. The goals should be clear and measurable so that when any individual committee begins to think about their objectives, they can make sure their objectives support the church-wide goals. In the HCI process, we prefer to have at least one of the goals have a numeric value that relates to reaching people for Jesus Christ.

For example, a church goal for outreach might be similar to the following:

By the end of [year], [church name] will reach more people by receiving five adult professions of faith, baptize eight people, and collect four hundred names from bridge events and follow up with them. We will also increase our average worship attendance by ten percent.

In setting goals, it is best to use the S.M.A.R.T. goal method to ensure they are good, sound goals. This S.M.A.R.T. acronym stands for specific, measurable, achievable, relevant, and time-based. Once a goal is written, use this method to make sure the goal is comprehensive and has clarity and measurability.

To start the goal setting process, start with the leadership team first. In this larger group, start with identifying goal topics. For example, the first topic might be reaching/outreach (see the example above). Other topics might include small group growth, changes in staffing, new ministries, different worship experiences, or all-church studies, to name a few. Once the topics are identified, break the group up into small groups equal to the number of goal topics identified. Each group will be tasked with taking the goal topic and developing it into a S.M.A.R.T. goal. The larger group comes back together. Each small group presents their S.M.A.R.T. goal to the larger group. The group then evaluates the goal to make sure it clearly articulates the group's desire for the church's work for the upcoming year and to ensure that it meets the S.M.A.R.T. criteria. Once all the goals (usually three to five) are presented, check in with the group to examine all the goals collectively. Ask these important questions of the group:

O Do these goals help us to become a more missional church?

O Do these goals create opportunities for us to live into our vision?

O Do these goals collectively look like they will challenge and stretch us but are also achievable?

O Are these goals what you, the leaders of this church, desire to adopt as the work of the church for the upcoming year?

If the pastor and leadership team can clearly answer yes to all these questions, the goals are adopted and ready for implementation.

The final piece of the strategic planning process is the objectives. The objectives are where the ministry is created and lived out in alignment with the mission, vision, core values, and goals. Many times, ministry is driving the church. In using this strategic ministry planning process, the mission and vision drive the church. Ministry is a function of helping us to be a missional church. The pastor carefully discerns which staff member or members are responsible for any given church goal. For example, identifying opportunities for professions of faith may come from a variety of ministries, so multiple staff members may be responsible for identifying these events (e.g., two from the children's ministry, two from the worship team, and two from the bridge team). The pastor works with the staff to develop strategies to complete the church goals. Using our same example, the pastor may ask the children's ministry leader what events might be planned that would lead children to the ministry and thus to be baptized. The details of the event are planned and executed by the staff person/team leader. Staff members/ team leaders are given the authority and responsibility for carrying out the objectives to accomplish their assigned goals within the stated budget. The pastor holds the staff (paid and unpaid) responsible for doing so. The pastor meets with the staff on a regular basis for updates, equipping, encouragement, and course correction. When the board/council adopts an accountable leadership model, they will then be responsible for holding the pastor accountable for the goals of the church. We will expand on this accountable leadership model in chapter 9. It will be very important to understand accountable leadership in order to implement and be effective with strategic ministry planning.

Strategic ministry planning is a driving force in a healthy congregation. It provides clarity of purpose and direction. Strategic ministry planning informs the rhythm and decisions of the church. It is critical for staff and ministry team leaders to know what is expected of them and their ministries and more importantly to know how their ministry is assisting the church in reaching more people for Christ. Strategic ministry planning creates the opportunity for constant evaluation and striving to live into the vision, which in turn continuously raises the bar of expectations and excellence. At the annual strategic ministry planning retreat, the previous year's goals are evaluated for progress before the next year's planning commences. Make sure the pastor, staff, and leadership take time to celebrate their accomplishments.

Case Study

For our leadership team, the strategic ministry plan retreat was the turning point in the HCI process. They had been present for all the presentations on church growth, studied the charts and the demographics...even tried to digest the bevy of books that I had asked them to read. They had attended town hall meetings and countless training events...but our time together, away from the demands of the world, was when it all came together. The purpose of the retreat was to develop the goals that would lead us to accomplishing our mission in terms of our own gifts and graces while being guided by our faith community's core values. As their pastor I had tried to articulate similar goals, and although they were receptive and kind towards my ideas, there was no buy-in or ownership on their behalf. That all changed when we "discovered" our path towards the mission together in the wilderness. Consensus bore ideas, which would quickly be written down as tangible goals...only this time we discovered those goals together...the team had ownership...the goals were ours...not mine. It was as if all of the preparation, the planning, the fact gathering, the interviewing, and the praying had come together at a single point in the process. We now owned, as a community of faith, a real path toward our mission. —Bill LaMora, lead pastor of One Spirit UMC in Kansas City, MO

Summary

	Compelling	Noncompelling
Leadership	Focus and clarity of purpose	Copy the calendar over from last year
Congregation	Knowledge of what and why of events	We've always done it this way
Community	Known, signature ministry	They have a plan?

Group Questions

1. What is the process in determining the activities and events of the congregation?

2. How are the events and activities tied into the church's mission and vision?

3. Are events, activities, and ministries evaluated for their effectiveness? How would you define effective?

4. Are events ever retired or do we just keep adding new events? Why or why not?

5. How do the staff and leaders strategically plan ministries each year?

Simplified, Accountable Structure

Prevailing Symptoms

In America, there has been a fundamental shift in how organizations function. We are no longer in a hierarchical, top-down culture that was pervasive in America in the 1940s and 1950s. Rather, today we find ourselves in a post-postmodern world. Most decision-making structures in mainline churches are not designed for speed of change. Rather, they are designed to manage. Most of the systems we have inherited were born in the 1950s for large, loyalty-based volunteer organizations. That kind of organization is designed to produce what it indeed produces. That is, it has produced an organization to be a representative democracy where everybody has a voice and a say—especially at the local level.

Many people thought that in this structure when we had multiple levels of decision making the risk of making a mistake was lowered. It was a means of quality control. The system was designed to preserve what we had. There has always been change, but the change was slow enough that the slow decision-making process was functional. By the time a decision is made using the older structure in today's fast-changing world, the decision is irrelevant. The old system places a high value on command and control. The new system values networking and information from all different directions. Many of our churches have leaders that grew up in the command and control world and are comfortable working in that system. These leaders grew up in times of war and General Motors where command and control was in play and working effectively. Leaders would rather make no decision than the wrong decision. The millennials have grown up in quite a different culture. The speed of communication and the availability of information have changed everything. Millennials would rather make a wrong decision than no decision at all.

The speed of communication and availability of information fundamentally changed everything.

Just look how quickly the word and act of a "selfie" came into existence. The knowledge and understanding of a selfie might not even have existed two years ago for some of us. And as of the writing of this book (August 2014), selfies are everywhere. Selfies are taken by multiple generations—not just the young people. Just think how quickly you can send a picture of yourself to hundreds of friends. A video of a family moment can be captured and shared with the world in a second with a click of the send button. This is an example of a new culture being introduced and the old culture embracing a new trend that has spread like wildfire.

All this is to say that if your church is still using the same decision-making structure that it was twenty years ago, there is a very strong chance it is not working well. There is also a strong chance that structure feels pretty cumbersome to most people (very likely for the millennials). In the old decision-making process, making decisions takes a great deal of time and multiple meetings. Because there has been so much change, many of us want the church to be the one place that doesn't change much. Therefore, we rely on tradition and the way "we've always done things" as our priority. Further complicating our decision-making process is our priority on fellowship and maintaining relationships with people we already know—even if those decisions cause us to not be missionally aligned. The congregation ends up being tied down by their decision-making processes and the value they place on fellowship with each other. If they are not careful, a congregation can spend enormous amounts of time in committees talking about ministries while at the same time saying they don't have anyone available to do ministries.

Despite hosting zillions of hours of meetings, we have encountered few churches in our consultations that actually hold people or ministries accountable for results. Most of the time we find that pastors have the responsibility for the church but have been given little authority to enact the things they think could help the church be effective. Most councils/boards manage a host of day-to-day operations and spend most of their time in fiduciary responsibilities. We have found very few that understand the concept of governance let alone accountability. Rarely have we seen a board participate in strategic ministry planning. Without a simplified structure in an accountable leadership model—in conjunction with strategic ministry planning—it is hard to see a bright future for reaching new generations of people.

Prescriptions

Example One

The church will move to a simplified structure with accountable leadership (as approved by the district superintendent), with new leaders and model taking effect [date]. This model makes more people available for ministry and traps fewer people in meetings. The current committee on nominations and leadership development will fill the new positions. The coach will provide the new leadership team with training on the simplified structure and accountable leadership on or before [date].

Example Two

The church will go to the accountability leadership model for the staff and structure of the church. Staff (paid and unpaid) and lay teams will set goals and be held accountable to fulfill those goals based on the mission and vision of the church. In this model, the board governs, the pastor leads, the staff (paid and unpaid) manage, and the congregation does "hands-on" ministry. If the consultation report is accepted, the accountability model will be implemented in the fall. "How-to" resources for this transition will be provided by the coach and the book *Winning on Purpose* by John Kaiser.[1] The lay leadership team will conduct a ministry audit on all current ministries by [date] to ensure that the ministries are in alignment with the new vision and mission of the church. If an individual ministry fails to align with the mission and vision of the church, the team has one year to realign itself or cease to be in ministry. The ministry audit will become an annual process.

The lay leadership team and pastor, in consultation with the coach, will put together a simplified structure. This model will be presented in the fall. The new structure and leaders will be in place by [date]. (United Methodist churches should see the policies in the *Book of Discipline*.[2])

Remedy

Training is the first order of business for a leadership team moving into a simplified structure. (See the HCI website for the training information.) In United Methodist churches, one of the biggest learning curves is learning how to

---

1. John Edmund Kaiser, *Winning on Purpose: How to Convince Congregations to Succeed in their Mission* (Nashville: Abingdon Press, 2006).

2. *The Book of Discipline of The United Methodist Church, 2012* (Nashville: The United Methodist Publishing House, 2012), ¶¶244.2 and 247.2.

simplify church structure. A second learning curve is understanding the concept of governance and accountability. Without good training and a thorough understanding of simplified structure, you will encounter a great deal of resistance. Sometimes we have encountered churches that don't understand the new systems and have already discontinued the old decision-making processes and therefore simply shut down the decision-making process altogether. It is as though they threw the baby out with the bathwater.

When you understand a simpler structure and the concepts of governance (policy versus management) and accountability, you will find that that understanding will motivate, unify, and move the congregation forward at a faster, healthier pace. The simplified structure model meets all of our *Book of Discipline* (*The Book of Discipline of The United Methodist Church, 2012* [Nashville: The United Methodist Publishing House, 2012], ¶247.2) requirements by placing four different organizational functions (trustees, finance, staff/pastor-parish, and church council) into one team of nine to fifteen people. However, going to a simplified structure model does not mean there are no longer any ministry teams who help manage and oversee the ministries of the church. We have seen multiple churches go to the simplified structure model and shut down all their leadership. This is not the point of the simplified structure. Quite the contrary, the simplified structure model is designed to empower the laity to do hands-on ministry and be involved in more ministry teams rather than committee work. The simplified structure model is designed to allow the nine to fifteen people to be more flexible, agile, timely, and coordinated with the decisions that involve the four primary organizational functions.

We are going to cover two different concepts here. One is the simplified structure model and one is the accountable leadership model. They are two totally different concepts. But we often move forward with both models concurrently. We rarely recommend moving to the simplified structure model without moving to the accountable leadership model. However, we have occasionally recommended churches move forward with the accountable leadership model without simplifying their structure, as accountability is merited no matter what structure is in place.

In a nutshell, the accountable leadership model is when the board governs, the pastor leads, the staff manage, and laity and teams are involved in hands-on ministry. If you are a United Methodist, you may adopt a simplified structure model, which combines the functions of trustees, finance teams, staff/pastor-parish relations, the church council, and other representative officers required by the *Book of Discipline*. The role of the simplified structure is governance. Along with the simplified structure, there would be a number of ministry teams that are responsible for implementing the objectives that accomplish the goals. These would all be tied together with the strategic ministry plan.

This is hard for a lot of people to figure out. Here is a metaphor I (Kay) have used to help a church understand how the simplified structure model works:

Imagine sitting around the table with all the members of the simplified structure. Now imagine there are four hats sitting in front of each person. When there is a financial issue of a governing nature that needs the attention of the simplified structure, everyone at the table picks up their "financial hat." Each person on the board is responsible for the final financial decisions of the board. Now a topic for staff/pastor-parish relations needs to be addressed by the board. Now everyone on the board removes their "financial hat" and replaces it with the "staff/pastor-parish relations hat." The same is true for a trustee issue. When a general governing issue needs to be addressed by the board, the participants put on their fourth hat, "council/board hat." Governing issues to be addressed by the general board might be hearing the goal update report from the pastor and holding him or her accountable for the accomplishment of such.

When the meeting is over, this is where it gets a bit tricky. If you are a trustee representative on the board, you pick up your "trustee hat" and wear it between board meetings. The same is true for the staff/pastor-parish relations and finance representatives. These teams of people (usually three representatives in each of the three areas) are responsible for the day-to-day governing issues that come up within their designated area. For example, if there is an employee issue that comes, the pastor may need some assistance from his staff/pastor-parish relations representatives. The staff/pastor-parish relations representatives would complete the annual pastor's review and share it with the board. (Reminder: in the accountable leadership model, the pastor has the authority to hire and fire staff as needed to accomplish the mission, vision, and goals of the church.) If the furnace goes out, a trustee is contacted. They are given the authority to handle the situation within the boundaries set by the board. If a repair costs under a certain amount, the trustees have the authority to carry out the repairs. If replacement is needed and is already in the budget, the trustee has the authority to carry out the replacement within any limitations set by the board about checking on cash flow or funding. The work of the three finance representatives will be to create the annual budget and take it to the board for review and approval. In other words, people are given permission to go about their job duties efficiently and effectively without having to ask permission. Authority is granted while holding the persons responsible and accountable. Those on the board who are not trustee, finance, or staff/pastor-parish relations representatives wear the "council/board hat" between meetings. Their focus is on the accomplishment of the mission, vision, and goals.

While there is no real need for setting a huge guiding principles document, there does need to be conversations that set boundaries. United Methodists already have a guiding principles document called the *Book of Discipline*. The conversation and resulting documentation that would be helpful for churches going to the simplified structure model might be around the following topics:

⊕ What is the maximum dollar amount that can be spent for unbudgeted building items without permission?

⊕ How many bids for building work are required over a certain dollar amount?

⊕ Is it standard procedure for the pastor to notify the staff/ pastor-parish relations representatives prior to any staffing changes?

Below, you will find a chart indicating our recommendations for where each piece of simplification, accountability, planning, and governance apply to different church sizes.

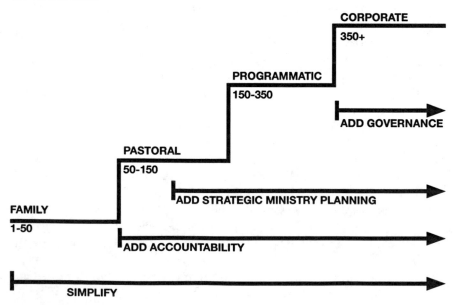

When the simplified structure model works, it really works. On the other hand, if you don't thoroughly understand, train, execute, and live into the simplified structure model with accountability, it can go very bad very quickly. Remember, many of us grew up in a representative system where everyone had a voice. This is a hard transition to make. Yet, in our new fast-paced world, it is a model that we must adopt and live into or we will get left behind. It is hard to imagine the decisions in our churches being made by only nine to fifteen people. Yet in our current structure there are usually nine or so people who already make the decisions. They are just dispersed among a variety of committees.

We recommend never moving to a simplified structure without also moving to an accountable leadership model. We use *Winning on Purpose* by John Kaiser as our primary resource for the accountable leadership model. This is a great resource for teaching and understanding who is accountable to whom and for what responsibility at each level of your organizational chart. The leadership team is accountable to Christ for the church being missional—"to make disciples of Jesus Christ for the transformation of the world." The pastor is accountable to the leadership team (board/council) for the vision and goals. The staff is accountable to the pastor for the goals and objectives. The ministry teams are accountable to the team leaders for accomplishing the objectives. The individual church participant is further engaged in more ministry with his or her own spiritual goals to accomplish. Remember, your church's core values are the boundaries that keep decisions in alignment with your mission and vision.

As a coach, I (Kay) first conduct the simplified structure and accountable leadership training with the pastor and leadership team. I also cover a suggested agenda to help them begin to move into a different model and conversation at their leadership team meetings. I have them hold a couple of meetings to try out their new skills. I attend a leadership team meeting to observe. At the end of their meeting, I go over with them where there are some possible times when they are reverting back to managing rather than governing. This is a hard transition for leaders to make, especially if they have served in leadership in the old model. I sometimes offer them the suggestion to adopt a word that would be a signal to the rest of the group when someone is wandering into a management conversation rather than staying in the governing conversation. Some leadership teams have adopted words such as, "[We are entering] tall grass" or "timeout." Management conversations are more technical rather than adaptive and easier to accomplish.

While downsizing the leadership team is a technical change, the real work comes in the adaptive change of moving into the accountable leadership method. The agenda changes. It is no longer based on reporting. The mission, vision, and core values should be printed on each agenda. This serves as a reminder and keeps the leadership focused on their accountability to Christ for the mission of making disciples. Other agenda items include prayer, spiritual development, approval of previous meeting's agenda, and updates on the goal progress from the pastor. The leaders should receive a packet of information a few days prior to the meeting with the financial report, minutes of the previous meetings, and any other pertinent information. This information does not need to be reviewed or discussed unless there are critical questions or issues to be resolved. This is also the time when individual team members can ask for help, recommendations, and additional information for completing duties the individual is unable to perform on their own (e.g., trustee issues).

At the regularly scheduled simplified structure meetings, there is no longer a need for committee reports. Since the pastor is being held accountable for the vision and goals, the pastor will provide a progress report on meeting the church goals. The objectives (day-to-day ministries and details) won't need to be discussed as the results of the objectives are wrapped up into the goals, thus leaving time to concentrate on the mission and vision—the big-picture work of the church.

Case Studies

Case Study One

Going to the simplified, fifteen-member board model has been transformative for our council. Community already had a unique board structure when we went into the HCI process, but going to the new model allowed us to clarify the governance function of the church council and kept me (as pastor) accountable in my leadership of the church. Because of this streamlined structure, the time to make decisions involving direction of the church has been decreased exponentially. Whereas it would have taken our former trustees, finance, and administrative council committees six months to a year to approve resurfacing of our parking lot, it took only two sessions of the new church council—one session to approve some research, the next to vote on implementation. —Kevin Shelton, pastor of Community UMC in Columbia, MO

Case Study Two

I would say the prescription that has the "potential" for the biggest impact is the fifth prescription, which is the transition from committee driven leadership to a single/accountable leadership board.

Our church (and especially me) was spending way too much time in meetings and not ministry. It was taking way too long to get anything accomplished.

For example, some groups would have to wait a month or two to get a decision because trustees meet in January and the next finance council meeting isn't until February, and administrative council was not until March. UHHHGGG! So frustrating.

The implementation of the simplified structure is taking longer to put in place that originally planned. There are many reasons for the delay...

- ⊕ Fear of great change
- ⊕ Perception that ONE board would RULE church
- ⊕ Perception that we were moving away from United Methodist discipline, as if Jesus and John Wesley came up with a committee driven system of government.
- ⊕ The need to seek "help" from other UM churches who have a simplified structure. This is very new to our conference.
- ⊕ Major church structure overhaul.
- ⊕ Need to train new leaders.
- ⊕ Need to get buy in from current leaders.

Over the last several months, we have accomplished buy-in from leadership. We have adjusted the time line for these reasons:

- ⊕ Training with our coach
- ⊕ Communication of change (the how and why)
- ⊕ Training of potential candidates for the board
- ⊕ Training of lay leadership team to pick board
- ⊕ Talking with other churches that have put board in place
- ⊕ Lots of prayer
- ⊕ Lots of one on one conversation

We are currently looking to implement:

- ⊕ A board that governs
- ⊕ A pastor who leads
- ⊕ A staff who manages
- ⊕ A church that does ministry and not meetings! Amen!

The results include:

- A renewed sense of purpose
- Fruitful meetings
- Focused staff and church
- Excitement!
- An increase in leadership base
- New young leaders stepping up
- Allowance for "career committee" leaders to transition out of leadership and into a specific ministry...Some willingly others not so much. —Travis Bennett, lead pastor of Morning Star UMC in Las Cruces, New Mexico

Summary

	Compelling	Noncompelling
Leadership	Clarity and purpose of role	The pastor has all the responsibility and no authority
Congregation	Decisions are easily received	Everything falls to the pastor
Community	Well-run organization	What church structure?

Group Questions

1. What is the process in your church for making decisions?

2. What are the criteria for making the decisions?

3. Who makes the decisions in your church? Is it working well? Why or why not?

4. Who is accountable to Christ for the mission? Who is accountable to the leaders for the vision? Who is accountable for the accomplishments of the goals?

5. Share a time when an opportunity for ministry was missed because the decision-making process was too cumbersome or time-consuming.

Chapter Ten

Staff Evaluation and Alignment

Prevailing Symptoms

You may think this chapter does not apply to you if you have limited or no paid staff. But quite the contrary, every church has staff—both paid and unpaid. This has been a new revelation even for us. As we work with congregations, we have learned there are a number of folks in any size church who lead the congregations. In the larger churches, those positions have become part- or full-time paid positions. In smaller congregations, there is still the same number of people leading. They are unpaid servants. So this chapter is for every church—not just large churches.

There are certainly major differences in how you arrive at leadership in a small church versus a large church. It is obvious in a small church that the process is far more informal or perhaps even an inherited role from previous generations. It is often even unspoken who is actually on staff. They may not even be in a named leadership role. But it is no less true that in a small church there are two or three leaders without whom that church's ministry would not exist.

It is true in a midsize church that you will have a combination of paid full- and part-time staff and a significant group of unpaid leaders. For example, when I (Bob) was at the Randolph UMC in the 1980s, we were running 150 in worship each Sunday. There were no full-time employees, but we had five part-time paid employees: a secretary, a janitor, a children's minister, a music director, and a youth director. Then there were approximately twenty-five unpaid leaders who were absolutely essential to the renewal of that church. Thirty-five years later, I can still name some of those leaders. They were that important to the advancement of that church and the kingdom. Our experience is that this staffing scenario is not uncommon for churches that have between 100 and 350 or 400 in worship each Sunday, depending on their resources. There is a significant combination of unpaid staff, part-time paid staff, and full- or part-time pastoral leadership in a midsize church. The most pressing responsibility for those unpaid leaders is actually doing their ministry and finding followers to help them in their ministry.

Dynamics begin to change significantly in a large church when it comes to staffing. It continues to be true that you will have a combination of part-time paid, full-time paid, and unpaid staff/leaders, but the combination shifts significantly. In a large church there is more full-time paid staff. The burden of carrying out the ministries falls more on the shoulders of paid staff rather than unpaid staff. The role of the unpaid leaders changes significantly, too. The most pressing responsibility of the unpaid leaders in a large church is to identify and recruit more leaders who then find new people to help them in their ministry. In other words, the primary responsibility of unpaid leaders is to raise up new leaders. The role of the unpaid leader can become a bottleneck as a church tries to transition from a midsize to a large church. The unpaid staff roles shift from getting followers to help with ministry to trying to get new leaders. It is a hard transition for leaders to make. Moving from midsize to large church is a much more significant change than moving from a small to a midsize church. When a church is growing from small to midsize, the role of an unpaid leader/staff still centers on getting people to help him or her with the ministry—in other words, to get followers. The only change going from small to midsize is that there needs to be five to fifteen unpaid staff/leaders rather than three to five. The role of the leaders does not change, only the number of leaders does. This is the bottleneck at this juncture of small churches moving to a midsize church. For those people who are used to a small-church setting, it is hard to imagine having twice as many people. We have also experienced leaders of small churches who have cried for years that they need more unpaid staff/leaders, but when new leaders come on board the existing leaders become fearful of losing their places. Sometimes, they even begin to sabotage the very growth they sought!

You may be wondering what we mean by paid and unpaid staff. For many years in the mainline church, we identified lay people who help lead the church as volunteers much like volunteers at a hospital. But something about that did not feel adequate to describe the importance of lay leadership in the life of the church. Certainly the word *volunteer* does not show up in the Bible. Using volunteer terminology makes it feel optional. It feels over and above rather than the normal way of life of a disciple. There were days when we even handed out volunteer pins and had volunteer luncheons. There is nothing wrong with this, as it was the church's attempt to show appreciation and thanks and add value and significance to this essential role. Then we went through a time in the 1980s and 1990s where we threw out the word *volunteer* and replaced it with *servant leader*. It was an attempt by the church to deepen the understanding of volunteering as a way of life rather than merely an option. It was also an attempt to align our language from not-for-profit volunteerism to a more biblical understanding of servanthood. This was moving from an optional volunteerism to the fulfillment of the expectations of a disciple or, as Wesley would say, "a way of living." The word *servant* is certainly more of a biblical term as Jesus said that he didn't "come to be served but rather to serve" (Matt 20:28). But in the American culture, the word *servant* really has not caught hold. We have trouble being a servant because it conjures up real emotional baggage.

Today, there is a movement in language to paid and unpaid staff instead of staff and volunteers/servants. There are three main reasons for this shift in language. First, the shift is a recognition that almost all of our paid lay staff in churches today began as unpaid staff at some time in their lives. This is true for most pastors, too. This is like a farm club system: raising up future leaders from our congregations to unpaid staff to paid staff and sometimes on to clergy. This is why leadership development and simplifying your structure is so important (see chapters 8 and 9). Secondly, by identifying paid and unpaid staff, the church empowers unpaid lay staff to work alongside paid staff with equal worth, value, and responsibility. And third, from the church administrative side, it makes accountability easier when everyone is treated as staff and therefore is held accountable for the results; it does not fall unevenly on the paid or unpaid part of being staff. For instance, no longer do we need to say, "I am just a volunteer," for this is sometimes a cop-out for mediocrity in our ministry. When everyone is staff, the expectation of excellence is high for all staff regardless of being paid or unpaid.

It is amazing to see the number of staff members who have no idea of their roles and responsibilities for their church. Furthermore, it is amazing how many churches are without position descriptions for their paid and unpaid staff. Or, if there are position descriptions, they are way outdated. It has astounded us how many times staff do not know the answer when we ask, "Who is your boss?" Lines of accountability and reporting are unclear. Or when asked when they are evaluated, they do not know or have never been evaluated. When asked how they would know if they were successful, most would respond, "I am still here, so I must be okay." Oftentimes in consultations, we have concluded that staff members are being retained due to being liked or preferred rather than for their competency, excellence, and effectiveness. We have also encountered many churches with varied expectations of the same staff depending on whom you talk to within the church. Job duties and responsibilities are unclear. We have found very little training to help staff develop. Staff meetings are mostly unproductive. On the other hand, we have indeed encountered some churches who have high expectations or their staff, have clear lines of accountability and authority, have productive team and staff meetings, and receive regular training and leadership development, which has led to a much high morale and an effective ministry that significantly enhances the chance for the church to grow numerically.

Many times staffing decisions are based on knee-jerk or panic reasons or on the desires of a minority group of people. Staffing is not based on mission and vision. Staffing is not based on the right culmination of people to bring the right blend of talents, gifts, experiences, leadership traits, and personalities. There is usually an urgent need and so churches often fill the position with an available person rather than keeping the position vacant until they find the right person.

Oftentimes a staff evaluation system is nonexistent (for both paid and un-paid staff). If it does exist, it's not based on alignment with goals and objectives that are aligned with mission, vision, and core values (see chapter 8 on strategic ministry planning). Many times we squash our staff's ingenuity and creativity by telling them how to do their jobs rather than by empowering them with the responsibility and authority to accomplish their jobs within the framework of the goals assigned and holding them accountable for doing so.

Often, churches hire staff to do the ministry for them. More competent and compelling congregations hire staff with an understanding that their main role is "to equip God's people for the work of serving" (Eph 4:12). Equipping is a more sustainable model rather than staff simply doing the ministry themselves as lone rangers. Healthy churches evaluate staff not only on their ability to carry out the objectives to meet the church goals but also on how well they build teams and equip the congregation to do the ministry.

In our HCI consultations, we see a lack of effective and productive staff meetings. Often, this leads to low morale and distrust amongst the staff. We have also run into churches that have irregular staff meetings or even none at all. In essence, the pastor is running around struggling to meet one on one with staff to keep everything aligned. This leads to a very unhealthy system. Even if there are staff meetings, they are often not productive and many staff dread attending them. This is a missed opportunity for leadership and spiritual development of our paid and unpaid staff. In most churches, we see the struggle to simply pay staff and thus there is no money allotted for training, team building, or leader-ship development. We oftentimes see small and midsize churches struggling to determine if they need either paid staff or unpaid staff, let alone have any leader-ship development in place.

Prescriptions

Example One

The pastor, in consultation with the coach and the three staff/pastor-parish relations representatives from the new single board, will evaluate current paid staff in order to align staff with the mission, vision, goals, and financial resources of the church on or before [date]. The pastor is given permission to restructure the staff in consultation with the coach in order to implement the mission of the church and achieve growth. The staff members need to understand their positions could be modified, repositioned, or terminated. New job descriptions will be developed as needed. The pastor will conduct annual staff evaluations. Staff meetings will be conducted every two weeks by the pastor for purposes of team building and ensuring transparent, clear communication among the pastor, paid and unpaid staff, and the congregation.

Example Two

The lead pastor, in consultation with the coach, board chair, and staff/pastor-parish relations chair will clarify staff alignment and the staff's primary job responsibilities.

Then all staff and ministry leaders will put together or revise their job descriptions with the pastor in consultation with the governing board and staff/pastor-parish relations chair by [date]. The pastor will work with the board to align all paid and unpaid positions with accomplishing the mission and implementing the accountable leadership model. The coach will spend a full day onsite on this process, [date].

To further the understanding and implementation of the accountable leadership model, the following will occur:

- The coach will work with the pastors and staff on the accountable leadership model and how it can be specifically applied.

- The coach will work specifically with the governing board on their role in the implementation of the accountable leadership model, in a workshop format, with date and times to be determined by [date].

- Leaders will learn to become proficient at developing leaders who develop others to be engaged in ministry for the sake of the mission. This requires the ability to teach leaders what staff has already learned about helping persons engage in ministry. The pastor and coach will

113

work with the staff to develop the training for these skills, which will be implemented by [date].

The pastor will assume leadership in mainly five areas, and these will be in his or her new primary responsibilities:

⊕ Preaching and worship

⊕ Staff development

⊕ Lay leadership development

⊕ Generosity development

⊕ Face of the church in the community (through service evangelism)

The pastor will assume responsibility for the following important areas:

⊕ Hospitality (front door, worship)

⊕ Connection process (getting people involved in the church)

⊕ Discipleship paths

⊕ Congregational care

A plan will be developed in consultation with the coach, and with appropriate leadership for each area of ministry to fully connect people to the life and ministry of the church.

Remedy

Only when the mission of making disciples is adopted, the vision cast, and the core values identified, can you begin to work with staffing needs. Before staff evaluation and alignment can be completed, the pastor and lay leadership must first have completed their strategic ministry planning process. You should never hire staff and fill positions until you do the slow and hard work to identify and define the mission, vision, core values, and goals. We want to hire staff that buy into the direction of the church. Otherwise, we get an undertow of people who are trying to do things they don't fully understand or buy into. After these steps are completed, the pastor and leadership are now ready to effectively determine both paid and unpaid staffing needs. After determining what staff is needed to carry out the mission, vision, and core values of the church, staff can be hired or aligned properly in order to live it out.

Underneath all of this is certainly a blanket of prayer. Changing personnel is very emotional and personal. Hiring the right staff is also personal and emotional. This process needs to be undergirded in prayer. It is not only important to understand somebody's ability but also to understand his or her spiritual gifts and personality. You can hire a very competent person, but if his or her personality does not mix well with the team and pastor, he or she will not be an effective hire. When changing long-term personnel (or perhaps even short-term personnel), it is very important to keep everyone in the communication loop. You cannot overcommunicate when trying to align paid and unpaid staff. You may recall us saying changing worship is a hard thing to do. Changing staff is the second most difficult shift in the church. Proceed with caution. You need to continually assure both paid and unpaid staff that they are good and valued people regardless of whether or not they can retain their leadership/staff position. This is just so hard. You cannot take this lightly.

To best align staff with the mission, vision, core values, and goals, the pastor and leadership need to consider the strengths of the pastor and needs of the ministries. As part of the HCI consultation process, the pastor completes the StrengthsFinder assessment, a spiritual gifts inventory, and a DISC test. It is also advantageous to have the entire staff do these evaluations in order to fully understand their leadership strengths as well as their leadership style. Here are some questions to consider when creating missional staff alignment:

○ Is your staff working in their sweet spots?

○ Are they working in the ministry areas where they have passion?

○ Are they team players?

○ Are they sold out for the mission and vision?

○ What training would be helpful for them to do their jobs effectively and efficiently?

Once the proper alignment is achieved, it is now time for the pastor to meet individually with both paid and unpaid staff to assign goals and collaborate on objectives. With the proper staff in the right positions, a pastor will now be able to share what is expected of staff members, but not to tell them how to do their jobs. To gain experience and create an apprenticeship process, we suggest the following steps for training:

○ I do. You watch. We talk.

○ I do. You help. We talk.

○ You do. I help. We talk.

○ You do. I watch. We talk.

○ You do. Someone else watches.

○ I go on to the next project.

It is in the Wesleyan tradition to apprentice people in ministry. John Wesley in the 1700s had an apprenticeship process in the "New Room" in Bristol. Frances Asbury, the first Methodist bishop in America, constantly had a young apprentice with him for ministry over about a six-month period of time. So apprenticing is in our DNA. It is our farm system. Not only is this a great way to mentor staff, but it is also an exceptional way to bring along ministry team members. Give staff the room to learn, be creative, expand their wings, and be successful. Not only is this a healthy and effective method to build staff, but it also means that pastors are teaching their staff how to equip and build their ministry teams.

It is important for the pastor to model accountability. Accountability for both paid and unpaid staff is a very new concept. The pastor and lay leadership will have to work overtime trying to embed a culture of accountability if none has existed. Understanding accountability will require a significant amount of time and teaching by the pastor and lay leadership—not only for paid and unpaid staff but also for the whole church. Remember, most churches have functioned with a very informal understanding of how to evaluate paid and unpaid staff in leadership position in a church. Many of the paid and unpaid staff have friends in the congregation, which makes it more complicated. The pastor will need to routinely follow up with staff on their progress on their goals and objectives achievement. Not only does this give the pastor the opportunity to check on progress, but it is also a great opportunity to encourage, equip, and make course corrections in a timely manner. When staff members know there will be a check on their progress, they are more likely to stay focused on their goals and objectives. If there is no routine check-in, they can easily lose focus and get off track. Accountability is best done consistently over a course of time. The worst thing that could happen is an erratic, on-again off-again attempt at accountability. Consistency is key.

Consistency is key.

A healthy church with an effective, fruitful staff devises opportunities to build cohesion within the team. Many churches often hold an annual staff retreat as a time for evaluating the past year's accomplishments, looking to the future, and working on next year's goals and objectives, in addition to leadership development, staff development, team building, spiritual formation, rest, and relaxation. A lot could be said about effective staff development, evaluation, and accountability. That is a whole book in itself. It is key to spend time investing in your paid and unpaid staff.

Remember, here are the key components to effective staff development. Some of those are the following:

- Morale

- Evaluation processes

- Alignment

- Staff meetings

- Personal check-ins

- Annual retreats

- Spiritual development

- Leadership development

- Accountability

The larger the church, the more time the pastor(s) needs to spend with the staff. Staff becomes the extension of the pastor's office if the church is to have a compelling, competent congregation.

Case Studies

Case Study One

The single largest line item of most any church budget is staffing. The typical church spends anywhere from 45–65 percent of its budget on its employees. Don't you think that sort of resource investment merits important time and energy? At Morning Star Church [MSC], we believe that staff are best developed in four areas: time together, evaluation, gratitude, and continual learning.

MSC staff begin each day together—meeting for prayer in our office at 9:00 a.m. We also meet each Wednesday morning for ninety minutes for Bible study and prayer. This time is invaluable, as it unifies us under God in our shared mission. And quarterly, we take a day off for a staff day apart. We close down the office and all join in on things like an outreach project, a tour of United Methodist institutions in the St. Louis area, or just a fun day floating down the river.

In terms of evaluation, we do annual 360-evaluations (which includes evaluations from a supervisor, a peer, a subordinate, and congregational members and a self-evaluation) each August and performance evaluations each January. The results of these evaluations contribute to the twice-a-month individual development meetings each staff person has with his/her supervisor (one meeting each month to discuss progress toward goals and one meeting to discuss personal development). In addition to personal evaluation, our staff takes a staff health engagement survey every twenty-four months. The results of this anonymous survey are shared with the staff/pastor-parish relations team, then the leadership team, and then the entire staff. After the five main areas of opportunity are identified, every staff person is appointed to a team whose purpose is to develop a two-year plan to address their area of opportunity. This creates engagement with staff, helping them own the work of making our staff as healthy and productive as possible.

Gratitude is huge. Everyone in ministry wants and needs expressions of gratitude. In my opinion, every staff person either deserves a huge "thanks" on a regular basis, or they need to be looking for another job! At MSC, we have found that including the spouse and family produces even greater rewards. Recently, we negotiated a deal at a local gym, and we provide a membership to staff and spouses, where the church pays half the monthly membership fee. Additionally, we plan two events or activities every year for the staff person and his/her significant other and two for his/her entire family. In the past, we've invited families to picnics in the park, and we've taken them to a local minor league baseball game and provided a buffet of ballpark foods and beverages. For staff and spouses, we do a nice dinner every year at a local country club, where we spend time together and cast vision for the coming year. Then we do something fun, like the time we chartered a bus, took everyone into the city for a great night that included dinner and games at a hip, cool restaurant.

Finally, development of staff means setting aside resources to develop each staff person individually. This will range from sending the staff person to a conference to hiring a personal coach. We also bring in outside experts to sometimes lead our all-staff meetings. Examples include a professional development person, who explained our DISC profiles and how we can learn to work with each other; a local personal trainer, who talked about the importance of diet and exercise; and a conference staff person, who coached us on how to have a successful personal spiritual retreat, something we ask each staff person to take quarterly.

In the end, we spent a lot of time and energy loving on and developing our staff, because at the end of the day, the ministry of the local church rises and falls with its leadership! —Mike Schreiner, lead pastor of Morning Star Church in Dardenne Prairie, MO

Case Study Two

Working with our HCI coach, my staff and I were able to engage in team building exercises that helped break down some barriers, and also to focus our staff on their gifts for ministry. My leadership was strengthened, as I was able to provide ongoing education and missional focus for staff beyond those initial coaching sessions. There has been turnover the past four years in several staff positions so that we have staff that not only are committed to the mission of the church but also take ownership in the process of reaching new people and making new disciples for Jesus Christ. The staff also knows that they are to help congregational members assess their gifts and passions for ministry and that staff isn't to do all the ministry of the church but to lead others to be in ministry. Staff is evaluated each year based on their leadership of others and how they make new disciples, instead of arbitrary metrics. I feel that the current staff at CUMC is a true team. —Kevin Shelton, pastor of Community UMC in Columbia, MO

Summary

	Compelling	Noncompelling
Leadership	Staff is equipped and aligned with vision	Staff is overworked and underpaid
Congregation	Staff is there to equip me for ministry	We pay staff to do the ministry
Community	Staff is deeply rooted in our community	We have staff there?

Group Questions

1. How do your staffing needs and evaluation tie into the mission, vision, core values, and goals of the church?

2. How are both your paid and unpaid staff evaluated each year?

3. What is your staff evaluated on?

4. Do we hire from within the congregation or outside the congregation? How is this determined?

5. Share a time when hiring, firing, or evaluation caused conflict within your congregation. Would better staff alignment and evaluation practices have eliminated or reduced that conflict? Why or why not?

Epilogue

We have concluded a couple of things in writing this book. The first is that these prescriptions are really the top ten principles for competent, compelling congregations. Second, we have concluded that these prescriptions are in the proper sequential order for implementation. When we started writing this book, we thought it didn't matter what order we wrote the prescriptions. But we realized that you shouldn't start at prescription six or ten. Start with the first prescription (chapter 1).

The first prescription is indeed the first prescription to address!

It will be important for your leadership team to evaluate where you are in these ten prescriptions (principles). When you have these ten principles working simultaneously together, your chances of having a competent, compelling congregation that is growing takes a big leap forward. Now we are not saying that in a given course of ministry that all principles will work at the same level each year. There will be some years that you will spend more time on some than others. But each one needs to be working to some degree at all times in order to be effective. Take some time to evaluate. Look at these sequentially. Don't move to the next chapter or principle until you have worked in the previous chapter sufficiently. You don't have to be perfect before moving to the next chapter or principle, but you certainly need to be fairly effective before moving ahead.

Throughout our work in HCI, we consistently talk about it being a process and not a program. A process is ongoing, whereas a program has a start and end date. While we believe this is a very comprehensive process, it is not perfect. If nothing else, this process gives churches a picture of current reality and creates a sense of urgency. We have also identified that the process works to the degree that the congregation and pastor work the process. The more fully engaged the pastor, leadership, and congregation is in the process, the better the outcome. If the process is treated like a program with a "to-do" list to be completed, the congregation may create some technical changes, but they will have trouble moving into the adaptive changes that leave lasting effects to create a healthier, more compelling, and missional church.

Coaching is everything! You can have an awesome consultation weekend experience, but if there is not follow-up coaching, the process will likely wane and not result in the desired transformation. In the HCI process, the coaching is more directive than other coaching relationships. That is, the coach's agenda is the prescriptions. The coach is tasked with holding the pastor, leaders, and congregation accountable for the implementation of prescriptions. The coach becomes a resource for the church leadership as it works to complete its prescriptions. Other times, the coach is called to conduct training and workshops to assist with prescription implementation. The coach's primary contact is with the pastor, but the coach also works alongside the staff, leaders, teams, and congregation. Our coaches check in with the churches at a minimum of once monthly. But we have found the more frequently the coach has contact the more effective the coaching. If your church decides to implement any of these ten prescriptions without a consultation, we highly recommend having a coach familiar with the process.

We would like to debunk a common myth that a healthy congregation is a congregation without conflict. Healthy congregations have some degree of conflict. If there is not conflict, there is a lack of pushing the envelope. A healthy congregation is one that has learned how to manage conflict—not necessarily resolve it. The health of a congregation is measured by how they manage conflict rather than how they avoid conflict. Bishop Schnase often says we believe that if we have a conflict at the church, it is a problem to be solved rather than a tension to be lived with. Schnase likens it to a rubber band. The only way a rubber band stretches is by creating tension. If you pull it too tight, it will break and snap back at you. The challenge is managing the tension. If you don't manage the tension/conflict effectively, you lose any chance of transformation. Conflict is required to get transformation. Transformation is not a science; it is an art. Transformation takes a great deal of walking along a tight rope, which takes a ton of courage.

We can't plant enough churches in American to see a revival. We have thousands of established mainline churches in America. We need some of them to find transformation if we are going to win back the culture for Jesus Christ. Be courageous! Be bold! Take the step in your congregation for transformation. On the other hand, it is okay for your congregation to decide this journey is not for them and to simply go into hospice care and become a legacy church.[1]

Competent, compelling churches create a culture of continuous improvement and evaluation. This must occur at every level. We must evaluate every ministry event based on the purpose, intended outcome, effectiveness, what went well, what we learned, and what improvements we can make. Paid and unpaid staff should constantly evaluate their ministries and how they can raise the bar of excellence in their ministry areas. The worship team should evaluate the worship experience weekly. Competent, compelling churches completely understand that standing still is the same as being left behind.

In monitoring churches in the HCI process, we have found the congregation's ability to work through adaptive change is directly linked to the outcome and sustainability of their prescriptions. In other words, if a church only moves through the technical change of a prescription without also deeply entrenching themselves in the adaptive change too, the church will likely backslide. That is, they will go back to the comfortable way of business as usual and lose the chance of sustaining transformation. Churches sometimes move through the transformation process and give up just at that ripping point of living into something new. Persistence for prescription implementation and creating a new culture and new way of being the church in the community is key for transformation to occur and have long-term sustainability.

While we are oftentimes impatient, we must understand that church transformation takes time. Transformation doesn't happen overnight. Transformation doesn't happen over a year. Most likely, transformation occurs only over several years. Many times, the consultation process and implementation are completed and the church does not see the fruits of their labors for a couple of years. It takes time to learn what needs to be done. It takes time to bring people along with the idea that changes needs to occur. It takes time to make the changes. It takes time for the changes to create results. Improved health takes time. It doesn't come fast or easy. It is important not to fix it all at once. Remember, too much tension will cause the rubber band to break! Transformation requires *determined patience*. If your church attempts these prescriptions, please implement in sequence, if possible. Many foundational things must be completed before other things can be built upon them. This is especially true if you are doing this on your own. We certainly advise against going about this transformation business alone. It is hard work! You need an outside voice to help with this. (See the appendix and HCI website for help.)

---

1. Read the book *Legacy Churches* (Saint Charles, IL: Churchsmart Resources, 2009) by Stephen Gray and Franklin Dumond for more information.

Determined patience is key to transformation.

However, church transformation is a process to behold. For when a church does the difficult and time-consuming work of transformation, God blesses their works. Joy, excitement, enthusiasm, and energy return to the church. The congregation grows, the leaders are passionate, the staff and pastor are working in their sweet spots enjoying their ministry, and the neighbors see the church as a vital part of the community. And above all, people are growing deeper in their faith and new people are coming to know Christ. For when all the pieces come together, this is the fruit of the works. So worth the journey! May you be blessed on your transformational journey.

Appendix

Below are the multiple components of the HCI process you will find on the HCI website (www.HealthyChurchInitiative.org). You will also find a list of contact information on the website for HCI coaches and consultants.

Healthy Church Initiative

Continuous Learning Communities

Pastoral Leadership Development (PLD) I

PLD II

PLD Next

Peer Mentoring

Lay Leadership Development (LLD) I

LLD Next

Consultation

Before

Self-study

Readiness 360

Mystery worshippers

MissionInsite

DISC

StrengthsFinder

Preconsultation workshop

Prayer team video link

During

Interview questions

Focus group questions

Spouse's questions

Saturday workshop

Sample consultation reports

After

Core values worksheet

Intentional faith development samples

Worship evaluation team worksheets

Visioning workshop

Accountable leadership workshop

Simplified structure workshop

Strategic ministry planning workshop links (www.amazon.com/strategic
-ministy-planning-workbook-kotan-ebook/dp/B0082E4K16)

Small Church Initiative (SCI) (churches with fewer than eighty in attendance)

Continuous Learning Communities (CLC)

Workshops

Peer Mentoring

Consultation

Workshop

Note: Many resources from the HCI process are used in the SCI process.

The companion workbook is a tool designed to help churches walk through the process of transformation. There is a handy checklist that guides you through the key components at each stage of the transformation process. The workbook will help keep you on track and moving ahead and will spark good conversation and communication in the journey. This is a must-have tool for churches working the process! You can purchase the workbook at https://www.cokesbury.com /forms/ProductDetail.aspx?VSL=175&pid=9781630885755.

CPSIA information can be obtained
at www.ICGtesting.com
Printed in the USA
FSOW02n2228260118
43846FS

9 781630 883157